D0536403

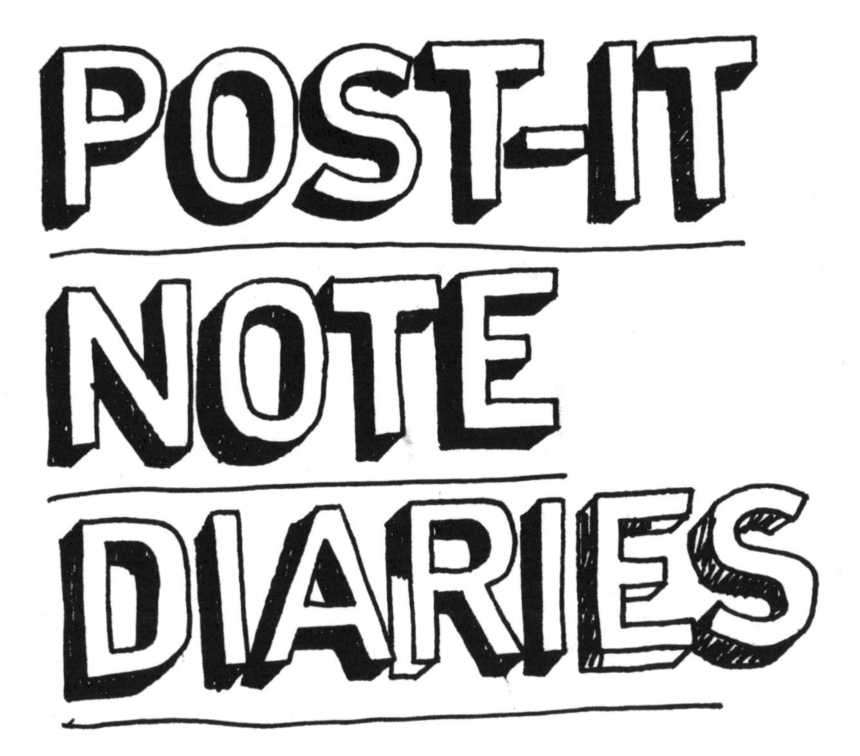
POST-IT
NOTE
DIARIES

20 Stories of
Youthful Abandon, Embarrassing Mishaps,
and Everyday Adventure

EDITED AND ILLUSTRATED BY ARTHUR JONES

A PLUME BOOK

PLUME
Published by the Penguin Group
Penguin Group (USA) Inc., 375 Hudson Street, New York, New York 10014, U.S.A. • Penguin Group (Canada), 90 Eglinton Avenue East, Suite 700, Toronto, Ontario, Canada M4P 2Y3 (a division of Pearson Penguin Canada Inc.) • Penguin Books Ltd., 80 Strand, London WC2R 0RL, England • Penguin Ireland, 25 St. Stephen's Green, Dublin 2, Ireland (a division of Penguin Books Ltd.) • Penguin Group (Australia), 250 Camberwell Road, Camberwell, Victoria 3124, Australia (a division of Pearson Australia Group Pty. Ltd.) • Penguin Books India Pvt. Ltd., 11 Community Centre, Panchsheel Park, New Delhi – 110 017, India • Penguin Group (NZ), 67 Apollo Drive, Rosedale, Auckland 0632, New Zealand (a division of Pearson New Zealand Ltd.) • Penguin Books (South Africa) (Pty.) Ltd., 24 Sturdee Avenue, Rosebank, Johannesburg 2196, South Africa

Penguin Books Ltd., Registered Offices: 80 Strand, London WC2R 0RL, England

First published by Plume, a member of Penguin Group (USA) Inc.

First Printing, October 2011
10 9 8 7 6 5 4 3 2

LIBRARY OF CONGRESS CATALOGING-IN-PUBLICATION DATA

Post-it note diaries : 20 stories of youthful abandon, embarrassing mishaps, and everyday adventure / edited and illustrated by Arthur Jones.
p. cm.
ISBN 978-0-452-29697-8
1. Diaries—Humor. 2. Humorous stories, American. 3. American wit and humor. 4. Celebrities—Humor. I. Jones, Arthur, 1974- II. Title.
PN6231.D62P67 2011
818'.602—dc22 2011006323

Printed in the United States of America
Designed by Arthur Jones • Set in Benton Sans

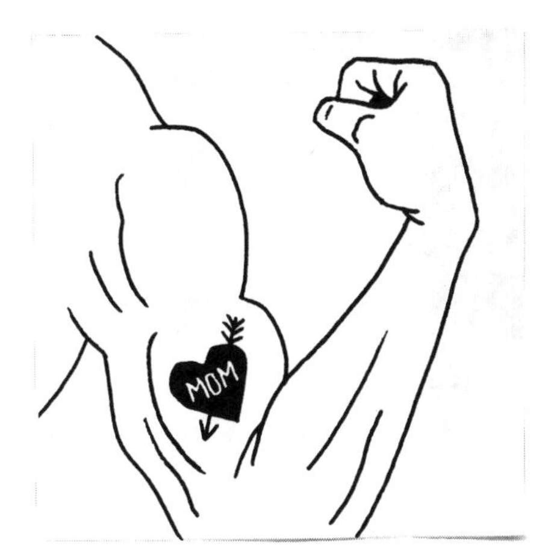

for my Mom

CONTENTS

FOREWORD

About seven years ago I worked at a Chicago marketing company performing blandly surreal tasks like color correcting photos of fast food and designing newspaper ads for supermarkets. It was a comfortable job and paid the bills, but when I was a kid and had envisioned myself growing up to be an artist, I never thought that would mean turning gray hamburger meat into brown hamburger meat with Photoshop or laying out coupons for cat food.

The worst part of having a boring office job is figuring out what to do with yourself during the most boring parts of the day—the sleepy middle hours of the afternoon when you've finished all your work but have to appear busy. It's during these moments—the ones when you find yourself theatrically shuffling and reshuffling papers around your desk, secretly playing online Scrabble, or stabbing pencils into your leg to stay awake—that you feel like you're blatantly wasting your life. To combat my workplace boredom, I got crafty. Using items swiped from the supply closet, I covertly made long garlands of linked paper clips, rubber band balls, and little sculptures of animals out of masking tape. These were small and silly gestures of defiance, but at the time I found them oddly empowering, like a prisoner making a shank from a toothbrush handle right under the oblivious noses of the guards. It was during one of these crafty moments that I started to obsessively draw on Post-it Notes.

Around the same time, my friend Starlee Kine, who was a producer for *This American Life*, invited me to participate in a literary event she was throwing as a good-bye party for herself before moving to New York. I wrote my story at my job, pretending to work on a spreadsheet document. I decided my story needed illustrations, so I made a bunch of quick drawings on Post-it Notes and scanned them. Later at the event, I clicked through a PowerPoint slideshow of the drawings as I presented my story. To my surprise the formula was a hit. The audience seemed to respond to the drawings specifically because they were on Post-its, something everyone uses.

Inspired, I kept writing stories while on the clock and slowly filled pad after pad of Post-its with drawings. A few years later I moved to New York, where Starlee and I started a literary event called the Post-it Note Reading Series. It was an experiment, where both established authors and nonwriters could present stories that I illustrated. Each show featured four or five presenters and a slide show of three hundred to four hundred of my Post-it Note drawings.

From the reading series comes this book. Some of the stories are new, some are old favorites from our shows over the past four years. I chose true stories because I felt they matched the medium. Post-its are used to communicate simple, direct, and necessary messages like "Sorry, I ate all your cookies," "Buy more toilet paper" or "We are breaking up," and I hope the stories in this book are just as blunt and recognizable to you as the canvases they are drawn on.

JOHN
HODGMAN

My Position on Subway Fares
by John Hodgman

Many people have asked me to explain my position on the New York City subway fare increase from $2 to $2.25. I am happy to oblige, and to do so, I present these two true stories that happened on two separate lines of the subway.

The L Train
It is not necessary for you to know how I came to own a small green staff with a large green Styrofoam cobra head on top.

Suffice it to say I was taking the L train last week, holding my cobra staff with the ruby-colored plastic gem eyes, which until recently I owned.

When the train reached Union Square, a gentleman, whose name I would later learn is Marcel, sat down beside me. And I could tell he was checking out my cobra staff.

This came as no surprise to me. In fact, the staff had been getting a lot of attention all day—people would look at it, and then at me, and then at the staff.

I know they were all thinking, "There's got to be some story here, about why he owns that cobra staff. Is he some kind of wizard?"

The fact is, there is a story, but not very much of one. And so it was then and there that I established my policy on the matter: You do not need to know.

But Marcel was a determined man. "That is really something," he said in a Haitian accent. "Do you know how much it is worth?"

As it happens, I did know. It was worth exactly zero dollars because I had no use for it, because I am not a wizard. Also, it was a very shoddy cobra staff.

It was just a cut-off piece of broomstick, and if there are grades of broomstick, this was the lowest, most splintery grade. And barely painted green.

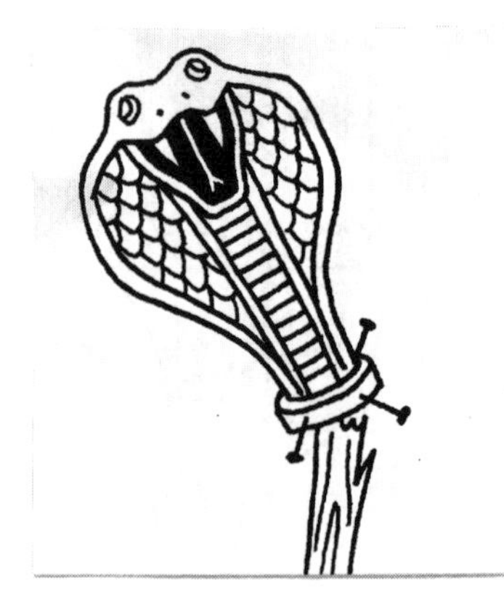

The snake head had been nailed on so sloppily that it offended my sense of craftsmanship. No one is making cobra staffs with pride anymore.

But I also knew that it was worth twenty-eight dollars, which was the offensively huge sum that had been paid for it by an actor friend of mine.

OK. Here is why I owned the cobra staff. This actor had bought it for a show he was doing.

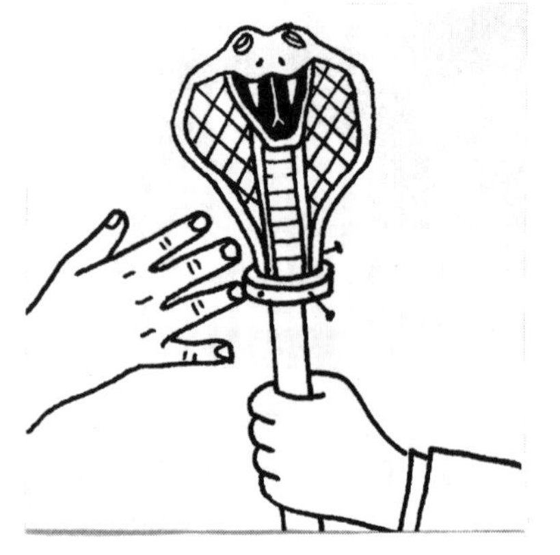

I looked at it and said, "That is really something," and so he gave it to me.

When I found out that it had cost twenty-eight dollars, all novelty value of having a cobra staff evaporated. I was disgusted, and insisted on returning it.

But he refused to take it back. In fact, he seemed relieved to be rid of it. I put it in my closet, and there it stayed, until today.

I told Marcel all this because he was still staring at it, as if hypnotized. That is what cobras do, of course: They hypnotize their prey.

"You should have it appraised," he said. And then he told me about a friend of his who had found a ring on the beach.

The ring was dark and discolored, but when he polished it, it was very beautiful.

And so he took it to be appraised, and it turned out to be worth seven thousand dollars.

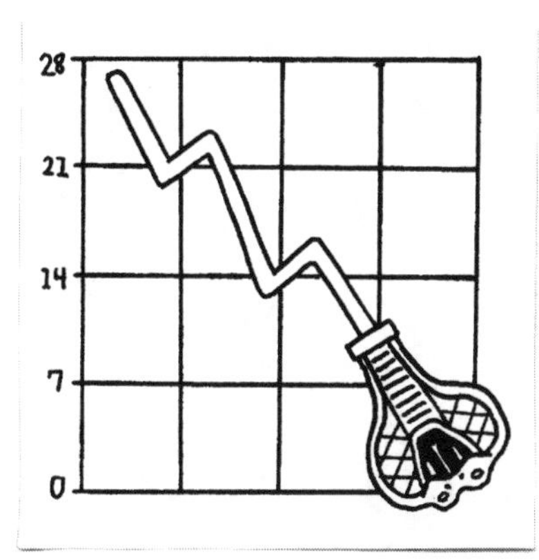

I told him that I was fairly sure my snake staff was not worth seven thousand dollars. In fact, my guess is that it could only have depreciated from its top value of twenty-eight dollars.

The once dramatic forked tongue had broken off in my closet, since it was made, I may have mentioned, of shitty Styrofoam.

And in fact I was now taking the train to Williamsburg to return it to the actor who had given it to me in the first place.

But Marcel said, "You don't know. You don't know. To me it could be worth five thousand dollars." Suddenly we were negotiating.

So I said, "Sold."

And he laughed and said, "No, no thank you, no. That wasn't the point." He said, "Things are worth different amounts to different people."

I knew he was right, because I knew that my cobra staff was worth zero dollars and twenty-eight dollars at the same time.

So I said, "Twenty-five hundred." But he said, "No, no, thank you."

And then Marcel said, "Maybe it will be on television. Maybe the actor will appear with it on a television show."

He was laughing again, but also serious, and even a little scared. He wanted it. The snake eyes had done their work.

And I said, "Believe me, if this cobra staff is ever on television, they will be lining up to pay me five thousand dollars for it. Take it now, for a grand. That's a steal. It's a conversation piece."

Which was true enough at that point. It was worth something now, to be sure, to provoke this rare and strange conversation. It was twenty-eight dollars' worth of snake staff, at least.

So when we reached Williamsburg, I said, "One hundred cash will take it away." But Marcel just kept staring, and then said in a kind of dreamy voice:

"My daughter will be very angry if it is on television and I did not buy it."

At that point, I probably should have just given it to him, but I didn't. Because I had become greedy, the snake staff became worthless again.

And, sensing that spell was broken, Marcel said, "No, thank you, no." Then my stop came, and we shook hands, and he told me his name.

We would never see each other again, unless, of course, one of us shows up on TV someday.

Meanwhile, I gave the staff back to the actor, who refused to take it, so we left it there, in Williamsburg, where perhaps it is still, waiting.

The Number 6 Train

When I first moved to New York, a ride on the subway cost $1.25.

I took the number 6 train to work every morning.

If you know your subway history, you know that when the Second Avenue elevated train was destroyed, in 1942, it left only one subway line on the East Side.

The number 6 commute became a massive, churning, full-body massage in suits.

One morning, I got on the train, and there were no seats. I was twenty-two years old, able-bodied, and college educated.

I knew I deserved a punch in the mouth more than I deserved the offer of a seat from a kindly stranger.

I did what I was supposed to: I didn't linger in the door wells, always moved to the center of the car, and maneuvered around my fellow citizens as they swayed and lurched.

I must have brushed the back of a young man who was standing facing the window, because he turned around and said, "Stop touching my back."

I said, "Excuse me." But the young man was not satisfied, now yelling, "Stop touching my back!"

I should point out, I had already stopped touching his back about a thousand years ago, or so it felt now as he glared at me.

And then he hit me. He lowered his hand from the strap and slammed his elbow into my jaw.

Seats opened up then, for sure. A woman screamed and moved away from him and he sat down.

I just stood there, bewildered, shaking, and hurting in the jaw and neck. I didn't move away; I couldn't. It was that crowded.

And so I stood there, and he sat there a few feet away, his head now in his hands, and no one knew what to do for a while.

When we reached Fiftieth Street he suddenly looked up and said, "I'm sorry." He wanted to shake my hand, and I shook his hand. He said, "I'm really sorry. Do you want to sit down?"

And I said, "No. I am fine. We all have bad mornings."

We rode together in silence for a while more, and by the time we reached Times Square he was crying.

In 1972 they started building a new subway line under Second Avenue. It was an enormous project, and they kept running out of money, until they finally just stopped.

There are still parts of the abandoned line down there, ghosts of tunnel and track. And every year someone in city government would say, "Let's get that Second Avenue line going again."

And indeed, they are once again digging on Second Avenue as I write this.

I am not so sure, though, that this is a good idea. Arguably if the train had been less crowded, I would not have been hit in the jaw.

On the other hand, without the human press of the city around us we would have gone to separate cars, never being forced to share that space, never getting to feel that blessing of apology and forgiveness.

In retrospect, I would say that was certainly $2 worth of subway ride. But $2.25? That, my friends—that is bullshit.

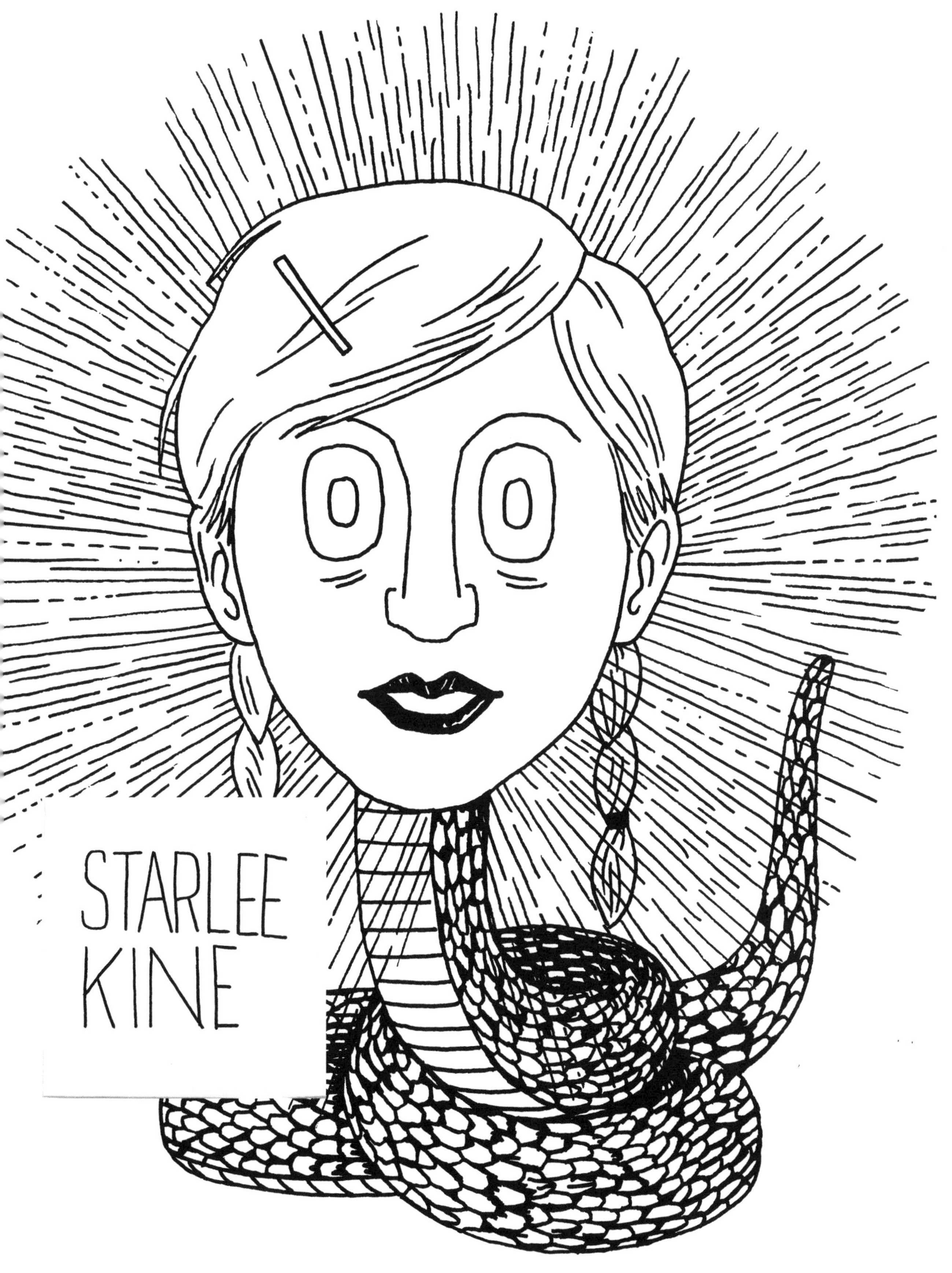
STARLEE
KINE

The Four-Minute Drug
by Starlee Kine

Some parents pass on cooking recipes to their children. Others teach them how to French-braid or sew on a button or crush the neighbor kid in soccer. In my family, my sisters and I were taught how to regret.

It was a trait my mom had learned from my grandmother, who had learned it from her own mom, and back and back it went.

For all I know, it started when my first ancestor lit a fire and then spent the rest of his life worrying about it going out.

As a result, I've always had a hard time with the concept of living in the moment. What, exactly, makes the moment so special?

There's a whiff of high school popular kid about it—loved by all for no real good reason.

In *The Silence of the Lambs*, did Buffalo Bill shout "Live in the moment" to the girl he stuck in that hole?

No; he said, "It puts the lotion on its skin or else it gets the hose again."

Even the most die-hard optimist has to agree that that was much more sensible advice considering the situation at hand.

The closest I ever came to living in the moment was when I was also living in Chicago.

Occasionally I would hang out with my friend Dave. He was the hypercreative, underachieving little brother of a successful fashion designer.

He was pretty paranoid and loved conspiracy theories. One night when we were out at a bar, he pointed to a poster of the moon landing and grunted.

"Can you believe they're still trying to sell us on that one?" he said.

He was so skinny that when it got hot he would wear a pillowcase with holes cut out for his arms and head and nothing else.

He lived in a loft with a million other guys and one summer they all pitched in to buy a wobbly Ping-Pong table that was on sale.

Dave turned out to be a sort of Ping-Pong savant, and he spent the next three months in his pillowcase playing nonstop with whoever was around.

Before I met Dave, he was a determined jazz fusionist. He aspired to be the next Jaco Pastorius, a legendary bassist who wore headbands like a folk singer but died young like a rock star.

Dave practiced so intensely that he injured his hand while playing his bass and had to stop playing.

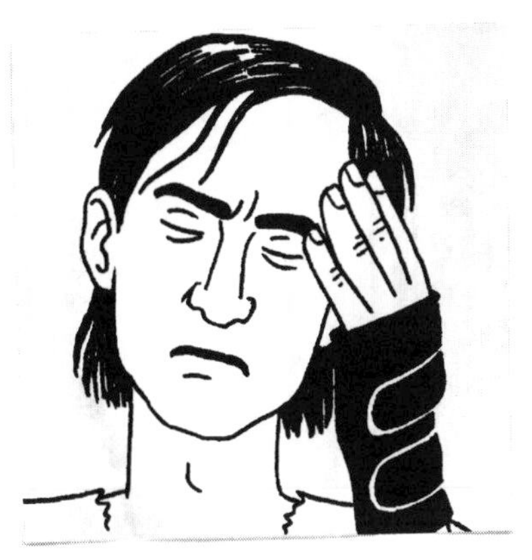

Depression hit.

He found a job suited to his mood at a local Laundromat, where with each towel he folded he could pretend it was the metaphorical towel that he was throwing in.

One fateful night, when he was taking out the trash, he looked at the Dumpster brimming with empty detergent bottles and instead of seeing a pile of trash, he saw his future.

He imagined a scenario in which he would gather up the bottles and transform them into life-size robot costumes. And that's exactly what he did.

Dave's robot costumes were definitely crazy, but somehow not as crazy as you'd imagine.

They were like suits of armor, complete with helmets and mitten gauntlets and breast-plates.

Only instead of metal armor there was plastic and instead of a family crest there were the words *Tide* and *Downy*.

In order to enhance the effect, Dave learned how to walk on stilts and soon he was showing up everywhere like that, to readings and rock shows and dinner parties.

Dave's driver's license had been revoked a few years before because he'd had an illegal ice cream cone sign on top of his car or something, so you had to go to his house if you wanted to hang out.

His building had the Odwalla juice warehouse on its ground floor and the guys always had crates of remainder juice in their fridge, even when they were at their most broke.

After investing in the Ping-Pong table, none of them could afford to eat for two weeks and they survived on nothing but fancy hybrid beverages.

Which might explain why they were all so good at Ping-Pong in the first place.

One night I showed up and Dave was looking more excited than usual. "There's something I want you to try," he said.

He led me into the living room, which was really just some old theater seats, a piece of wood on cinder blocks for the computer, and a filing cabinet.

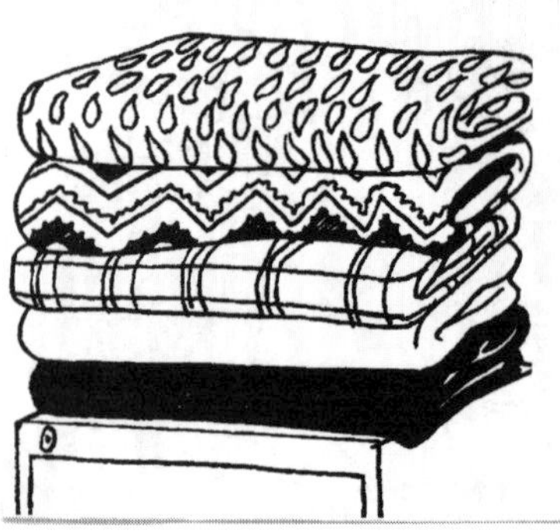

On top of the filing cabinet was a stack of three carefully folded knit afghans, which I noticed because they were the one small, dear attempt at domesticity in the entire place.

Dave went to the desk, withdrew a Ziploc bag, and held it out to me.

"It's a four-minute organic drug that I ordered off the Internet," he said. "It lasts exactly four minutes."

"Then you go back to just how you were before. There aren't any physical side effects or anything. And it'll change your life."

"In four minutes?" I asked.

"It's a very intense four minutes."

"But what can possibly even happen in that time?"

Just then Dave's roommate, Robroy (real name, one word) popped his head in. "Are you guys talking about the four-minute drug? It's great; you're going to love it."

He told me that when he took it, he was whisked to a bright green field. As Robroy the adult hovered above, Robroy the boy enjoyed a picnic lunch on the ground below with their mom.

They spread soft cheese on slices of bread and were about to start layering on the prosciutto when Robroy was whisked back to the loft.

He said it was the most peaceful four minutes of his life.

Dave nodded enthusiastically. "Totally! *Totally!*" he kept saying, even though his own experience had been nothing like that.

When he took the drug, he simply entered the wall next to his bed and stayed there until the four minutes were up.

Then he repacked his bowl and tried to enter the wall again, but much to his frustration he kept getting whisked away to other, more exotic hallucinations.

Once, he found himself on a deserted island seeking advice from a chimp.

Another time he was underwater and had gills.

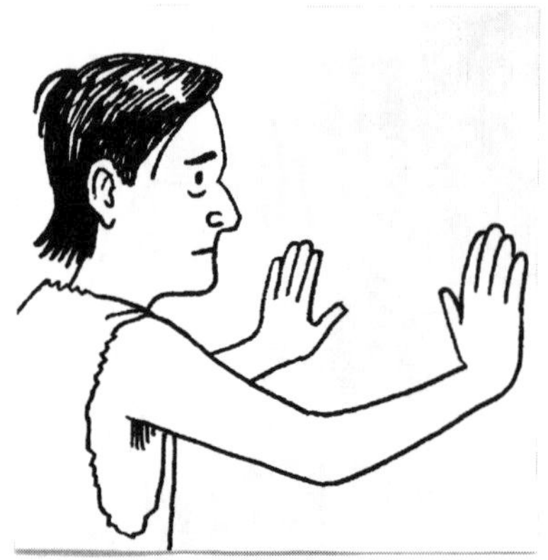

Dave wasn't interested in any of that. He just wanted back into that wall.

That day, he packed and repacked his bowl eight separate times, but thirty-two minutes later he was right back where he had started.

Just your average robot-costumer conspiracy theorist who had to settle for being adjacent to walls like everybody else.

Now, in the living room, Dave offered his pipe to me.

I took it right away, not because I was so curious to try it but because I was in a hurry to get it over with.

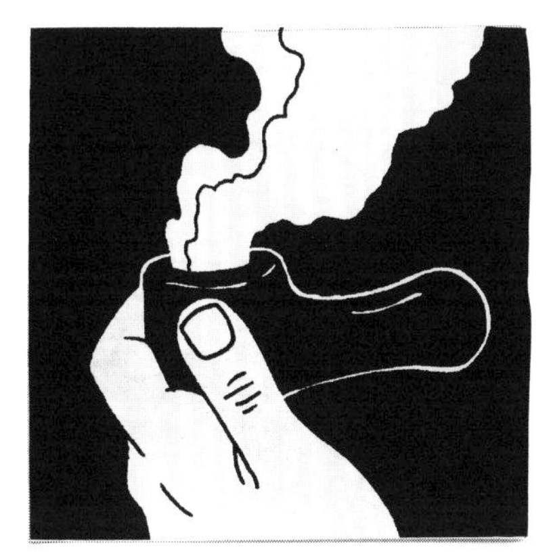

I have no problem with most of the aspects of drug taking.

The health risks and the economic ruin.

The lying and the stealing.

The nodding off in public.

The breaking up of the band.

The dipping of a track-marked toe into the disease-ridden waters of prostitution. That all seems fine.

It's the actual experience that I could do without. Which is why taking this drug seemed, to me, like a win-win situation. I'd only have to "experience" it for four minutes and I'd still get credit.

The second I inhaled, something told me it was working. Perhaps it was because I could no longer sense who I was or what life had been like at any point before.

Or maybe the tip-off was that the computer's screen saver had transformed into an evil, mocking face.

The afghans on top of the filing cabinet were now monsters and the faded paisley rug on the floor had come to life and promptly begun to eat Dave.

Dave later told me that I kept repeating, "Oh this isn't good; this is not good."

He said at one point I turned to the afghans and hissed, "So we meet at last!"

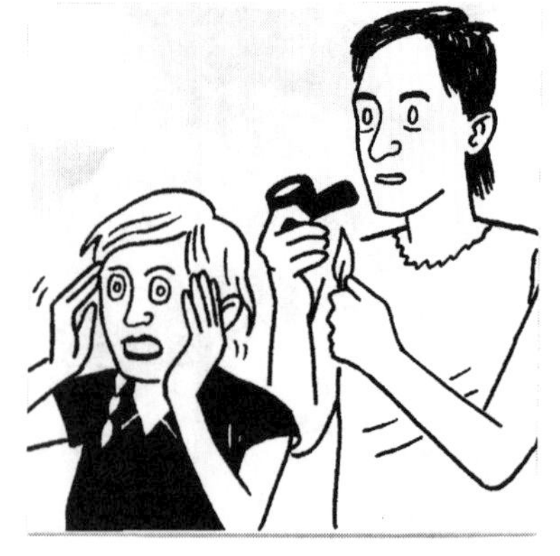

He hadn't anticipated this reaction at all and was naturally worried. And so he did the only thing he could think of to help. He fired up another bowl.

"I'm coming in after you," I heard him say, but it was so faint, so far away.

Next thing I knew Dave was diving into the rug as though it were the sea. He disappeared for a second, and then popped his head back out, gasping for air.

I reached out my hand and he tried to make his way toward me, but the waves were just too choppy.

Then he grew a beard, the afghans reared up for the kill, I saw sharp teeth, and the screen saver laughed and laughed.

I was sure it was all over for us both.

Then just as quickly as it had started, it stopped. My identity came rushing back. I could again conceptualize space and time.

If Robroy had chosen to take the four-minute drug right then, this is what he would have seen as he hovered above:

Me curled up on my chair, trying to make sense of the thrashing, flailing, dog-paddling Dave on the rug below.

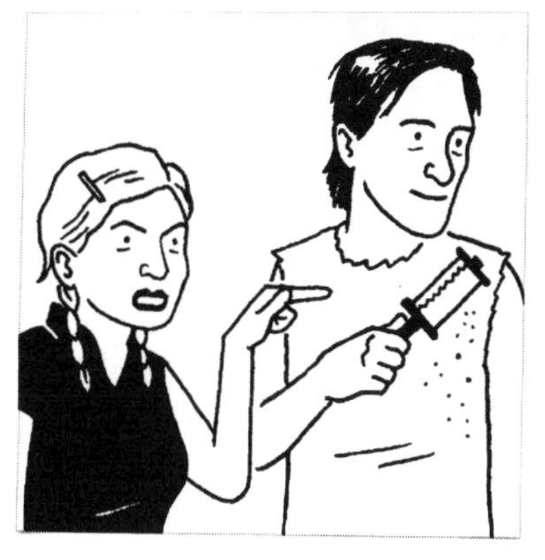

"That was the worst four minutes of my life," I told Dave once he'd recovered and dusted the lint from his pillowcase.

We went into the kitchen, where Robroy handed me a bowl of white rice and then the two of them asked me question after question about what it was like to not enjoy drugs.

Until meeting me, it had never occurred to them that such a thing was possible.

I answered as best I could, using props when words wouldn't suffice: the saltshaker as me, the pepper mill as Dave, an empty Odwalla juice bottle as the screen-saver demon.

There was a definite vibe of sweaty accomplishment in the air; I'd lived through living in the moment . . . and survived. Now all I had to do was make sure it didn't happen again.

ARTHUR
BRADFORD

Alaska Death Trip
by Arthur Bradford

Upon graduation from high school I teamed up with two friends, Matt and Fred, and we decided we would make our fortunes working in the fish-canning factories of Alaska.

Our plan, such as it was, consisted of driving from our homes in New England across Canada, and then into the wild Alaskan frontier.

None of us owned a reliable vehicle, so I convinced my grandmother to lend us her old Jeep Wagoneer.

We all met up at Grandma's house one night and after dinner we decided we should hit the road then and there.

It was late and my grandmother urged us to spend the night and leave in the morning, but we were having none of that. We were too excited.

The open road awaited us! Those fish canneries were calling our names!

We left around midnight and soon ran out of gas.

All the gas stations were closed at that hour so we spent that first night in the Jeep only a few hours from where we had started.

In the morning we filled our tank and crossed the border into Canada. That setback with the gas gave us an idea: Why stop moving?

We could just rotate drivers and sleep in the Jeep all the way to Alaska. We'd make great time!

We sped past the Great Lakes, stopping only for short meals and bathroom breaks.

A driving hierarchy was established. Matt was the best driver, so he drove for the longest stretch, usually well into the night.

He'd wake me up around dawn and I'd sleepily take the wheel. I remember waking at dawn at the foot of the great Canadian Rocky Mountains.

Matt handed me the wheel and before he went to sleep in the backseat he said, "Look out for the rabbits." I was confused at first, but then as I drove, I saw what he meant.

There were rabbits all over the road, hundreds of them. Something about the heat of the asphalt had drawn them there.

I tried to drive around them or slow to a crawl, but they just darted under the tires.

I kept hearing these awful little *thuds*. It was ridiculous, like they were bent on suicide.

Finally I stopped driving and yelled at them, "Get off the road! Fucking rabbits!" This didn't help.

Fred was the worst driver of our group. Matt and I would try to sleep while he careened down the mountain roads, but we kept banging our heads on the sides of the Jeep or falling off the seats.

Fred loved to accelerate and then hit the brakes once he realized things were going too fast. It was a poor driving technique. Even so, we were making great time.

We soon reached the Yukon, home of the mythical midnight sun. It never gets dark there!

The border crossing back into the U.S. was just a little set of trailers and a makeshift toll bar across the road.

The border patrol agent asked us if we had any guns or weapons to declare and we replied that we did not.

I remember wondering if we should have weapons to declare. This was the frontier, after all.

Then the border agent asked, "Do you have any drugs or drug paraphernalia to declare?" "No," I said, "we don't."

I suppose I wasn't very convincing on this point. The agent said, "Please step out of your vehicle."

They searched the Jeep and found a two-foot-long water pipe, also known as a bong, and a bag of weed.

I thought we would be arrested on the spot, but instead, the penalty for our crime was the seizure of our vehicle.

The nearest town was a hundred miles away, a little Alaskan village called Tok. The irony of that name was not lost on us, by the way.

The only way to get a ride out of there was to split up. Alaska is a terrible place to hitchhike, we soon learned, because there's no such thing as a short ride.

If you pick someone up, that person is with you for hours—days, even.

After hours of rejection, I finally caught a lift to Tok with a Canadian fur trapper named Bill.

Matt and Fred arrived a little later in the back of a border agent's truck, sandwiched between two big huskies.

Tok stood at the divergence of two roads along the Alaska Highway. One led to Anchorage, and the other to Fairbanks. Each city was about ten hours away.

We were stuck there for nearly a week and it rained the entire time.

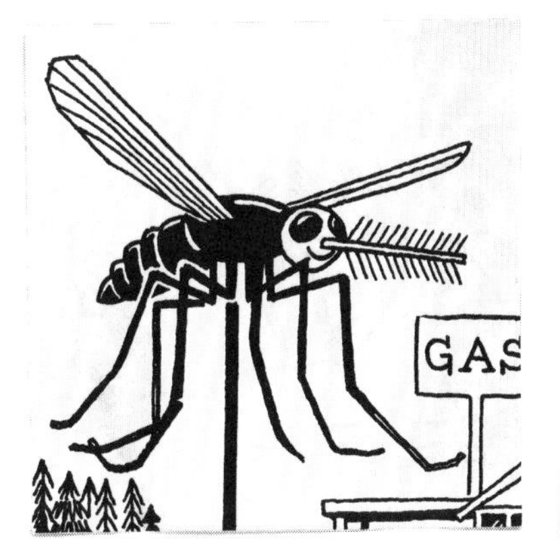

A local gas station had built a statue of the world's largest mosquito.

This might have been amusing to us if we hadn't been sleeping in tents each night and getting attacked by the real things.

The mosquitoes up there are enormous, like flying syringes.

After the Jeep was seized I placed a phone call to my grandmother. I told her the good news was that we had made it to Alaska.

"The bad news," I said, "is that when we reached the border they found some marijuana and a pipe in the vehicle."

There was a confused silence on the other end of the line. "Now how did that get there?" she asked.

My poor grandmother was honestly wondering if perhaps one of her acquaintances had dropped the drugs in her Jeep on some earlier occasion.

I set her straight, however.

We pinned our hopes of escape on a legal loophole: The Jeep belonged to my grandmother, and since she'd had no knowledge of our drug smuggling, she might be allowed to have it back.

My grandmother signed some papers and faxed them to a lawyer in Anchorage who, after nearly a week of haggling, somehow got this logic to stick.

Much of our time in Tok had been spent waiting around in the town's one bar.

When we learned that the Jeep had been released we offered one of our drinking companions twenty bucks and a radio cassette player to drive us back to the border so we could retrieve it.

This man, who was known as Eric the Eskimo, traded the radio to the bartender for eight beers, so we didn't end up leaving until 2:00 a.m.

The Jeep had been sitting in a dirt parking lot at the border for more than a week.

When we arrived and opened the door an amazing puke-inducing odor of spoiled ham, old socks, and rotten milk assaulted us.

Matt and I opted to ride back to Tok with Eric the Eskimo, while Fred braved the stench and drove the Jeep.

The rain had ceased and a beautiful misty morning emerged as we got under way. We were finally back on the road and I recall thinking that now, at last, our luck might change.

Speeding along in the Jeep ahead of us, Fred reached down to the floor to find a new cassette for the tape player.

The wheels of the Jeep drifted into the soft sand shoulder.

Fred popped his head up and slammed his foot on the brake.

The Jeep swerved and then began an incredible series of cartwheels, flipping end over end across the barren highway.

When it finally came to a stop the Jeep lay on its side, tires spinning, smoke rising from the crumpled hood.

"Oh Jesus," said Eric. I just sat there repeating, "No, no, no . . ." I thought Fred might be dead.

But then Fred climbed up out of the Jeep's window, rubbing his head and cursing repeatedly. "Shit. Fuck. Shit. Fuck." He kept saying that over and over.

He was fine, though, except for a bump on the back of his head. Of all the dumb shit we had done on that trip, at least we'd made a habit of wearing seat belts.

Eric said, "You boys are lucky to be alive. All of you."

But we didn't feel lucky at all. We spent an hour and a half cleaning up all the crap on the highway.

Bits of glass, ripped up tires, clothing, broken fishing rods—it was scattered everywhere for hundreds of feet.

There were big divots in the road at each spot where the Jeep had come down. I surveyed the scene and stood amazed at the degree of destruction we had wrought upon this land.

The whole time we were out there cleaning up that mess only one vehicle passed by, a long haul trucker who radioed the state police.

Eventually a big tow truck came along and hauled the wrecked Jeep's carcass away. "There it goes," I thought to myself.

We all got into Eric's car and drove back to Tok's only bar in silence.

It was barely 8:00 a.m. when we arrived, but there were several patrons already drinking and we joined them.

We never did make it to the fish canneries that summer. We painted houses in Anchorage instead, and as soon as we'd amassed enough cash to fly home, that's what we did.

I think that was the time I learned about limitations, if this makes sense—that there are indeed consequences for our actions.

It seems like an obvious lesson, but I'm pretty certain I didn't know it at the time. And it wasn't a bad way to learn it.

Every so often I think it's OK, even good, to crash and burn, especially when you are young and might gain something from it.

Eight years later, my friend Matt, the good driver, died in a spectacular rock climbing accident on the great wall of El Capitan, in Yosemite.

He'd become a world-class climber and I suppose the whole idea of limitations and consequences never really settled in his mind.

Interestingly, Fred, the poor driver, is now a brain surgeon—a really good one, apparently.

He performs delicate lifesaving operations at one of the most prestigious hospitals in the world.

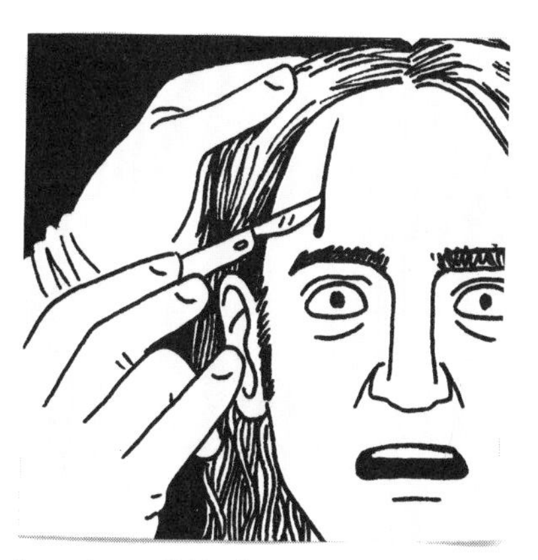

I'm not sure I'd let him at the inside of my brain, though, to be honest.

MARY
ROACH

How to Not Have Sex with Nicolas Cage by Mary Roach

Many years ago, I had a brief, ill-fitting career writing celebrity profiles.

I worked for one of those skinny newsprint magazines that is stuck inside the Sunday paper and consists mainly of ads for collectible dolls and items from the Franklin Mint.

One of my first interviews was with Nicolas Cage.

I met Mr. Cage in the hallway outside his apartment, on the top floor of an old municipal building in downtown Los Angeles.

He was taller than I had expected and less happy to see me.

I recall approaching my first few interviews with the idiotic expectation that the celebrity and I might have so much fun together that we'd become pals.

We didn't go inside the apartment because Mr. Cage was hungry and wanted to go get something to eat.

We drove to dinner in a Lamborghini that he had parked downstairs.

This kind of car is unusual in that the doors open up, not out, as though the assembly line workers had come in drunk and installed trunk lids where the doors were meant to go.

The body of the car was low and awkward to get into, like that cramped metal pod that takes tourists to the top of the St. Louis Gateway Arch.

I told Mr. Cage that I drove a 1966 Volvo 122S. "Oh, the one in *The Saint*!" he said approvingly.

The guy in *The Saint* drove a snappy Volvo sports car with fins.

"No, not that one." My car was a sedan. It needed a running start to make it up a moderate hill.

There was traffic. The Lamborghini sounded like it was in the wrong gear.

"It's like a pit bull on a leash," said Mr. Cage. "It just wants to go."

Finally a few car lengths opened up in front of us, and Mr. Cage shifted gears.

"We're pulling g's here!" he yelled. My stomach wrapped around my spine.

For the first time since we'd met, Mr. Cage seemed happy. Though without actually smiling.

Soon the car slowed again. Mr. Cage needed the kind of city streets that exist only in car commercials, with no one else on them.

After another mile or so, we turned in to the driveway of a steakhouse identifiable at some distance by a life-size plastic cow atop a sign pole.

I tried to get some banter going about the plastic cow, but it didn't take.

We were seated right away. Mr. Cage walked to the booth with his head turtled low between his shoulders, to avoid notice. He said it had become a reflex.

At one point we got onto the topic of Mr. Cage's new aquarium.

Because I was a terrible and self-absorbed interviewer, I cut him off and began talking about the aquarium I'd kept in junior high.

Mr. Cage ate his T-bone steak and listened politely.

"There was a snail infestation," I said. "Little ones, and tons of their eggs—all over the glass. After a while I couldn't stand it."

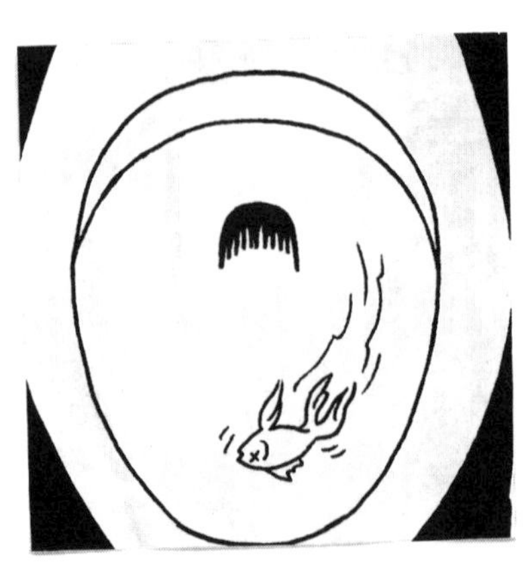

"I flushed the fish down the toilet."

Mr. Cage's aquarium was larger than mine had been, and there was a person who helped with it, presumably taking care of things like snails.

One of the creatures in it was an octopus. "They're really smart," he said.

"If octopuses got along with each other, which they don't, they would rule the ocean."

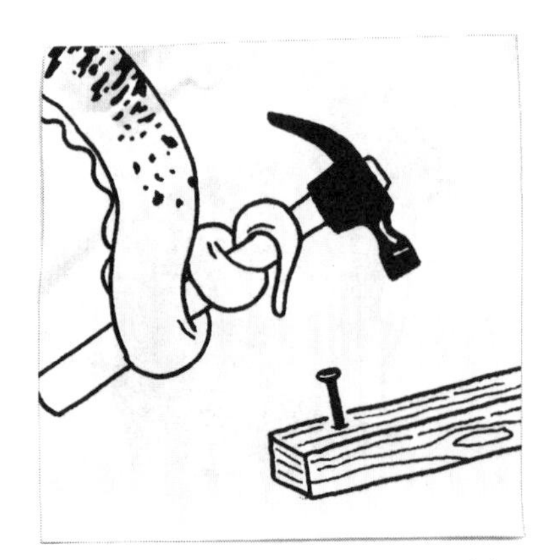

"They have all those appendages and they can build things."

I regret now that I did not ask what octopuses build.

Instead I asked him if *he* could build things. I actually said: "Do you own any power tools?"

Mr. Cage said that he owned a saw. "For making things with my son. But it's a handsaw."

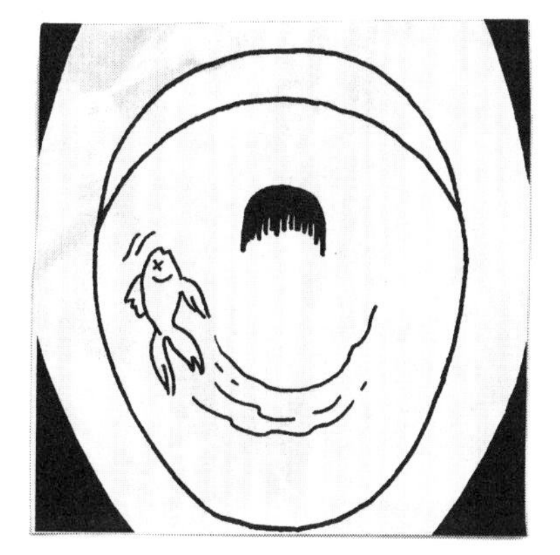

Then he said, "You flushed your fish down the toilet?" I confirmed this fact.

"Sorry. Who am I to judge?" I thought that was the end of it, but it wasn't. "It isn't the best thing to do with your animals, is it?"

"I mean, you could have returned them to the pet store, probably."

It was seeming like we weren't going to become friends.

We drove back to the parking lot where I'd left my rental car.

It was easy to find because it was the only one left in the lot.

This was because the lot had closed at 7:00 p.m. A large metal gate had been rolled across the driveway.

I recalled that Mr. Cage had asked me when we pulled away whether this was a late-night lot, and that I had, God knows why, answered yes. He didn't bring this up.

"OK. Well. Do you want to stay at my apartment?"

I vividly recall this moment.

The Lamborghini was idling, though nothing about the sound it was making suggested idleness.

Across the street was a sign for a restaurant that featured menudo.

I tried to remember which organ menudo was, at the same time as I tried to grasp the implications of Mr. Cage's offer.

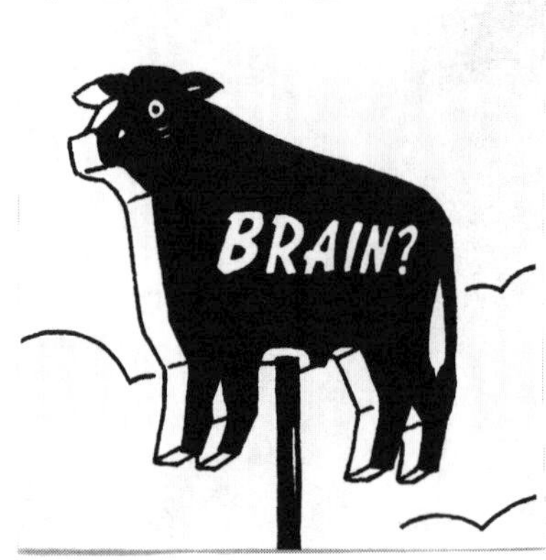

Brain?

Stomach?

Will I sleep on the couch?

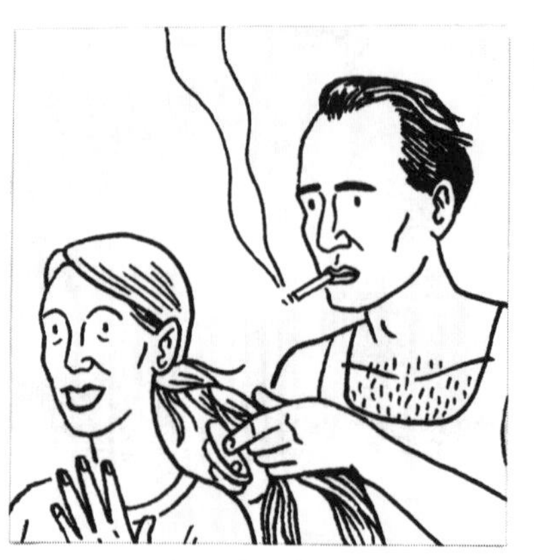

Will we stay up late talking?

Stomach lining!

Plus it's a Latino pop band.

How interesting to name a band after a cow's stomach lining.

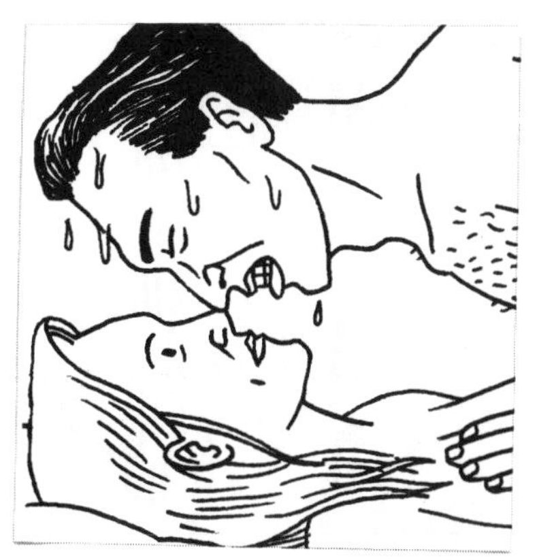

Are Nicolas Cage and I going to sleep together?

This seemed unlikely, what with the fish murders and the utter absence of flirting or any indication of interest on his part.

Mr. Cage let me into the apartment. The walls were painted mauve with panels of leopard print.

I had seen the same unusual combination on the exterior of an antique shop in San Francisco, on Guerrero Street, and wondered if that was where he'd gotten the idea for his decor.

The couch was dark green leather and large, the kind that turns corners.

There was some awkwardness.

"Where do you want me to sleep?" I said.

He smiled. He seemed to find this question funny

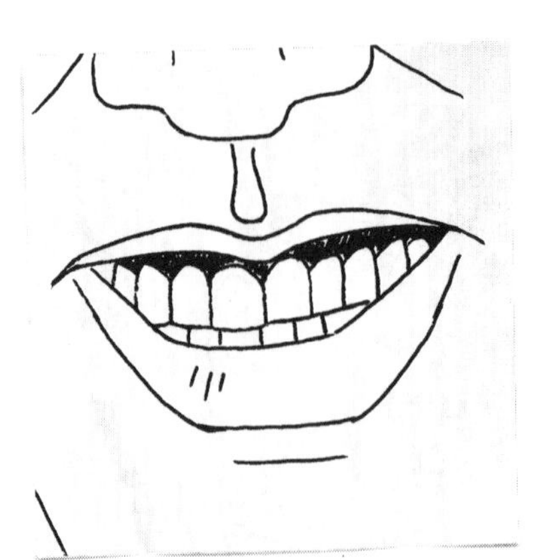

I think it was the first time that evening that I had seen his teeth.

He pointed to the bedroom. "I want you to sleep in here. This is where I want you to sleep."

Then he walked back to the front door. He was going to his house in the hills, the house he shared with Patricia Arquette and the smart octopus.

It hadn't occurred to me that a person would have two places to live in one city. "Make yourself at home," he said, and left.

It was clear Mr. Cage didn't spend much time in the apartment.

The refrigerator was empty except for a bottle of Chalk Hill chardonnay, some Hershey's syrup, and a spray can of Pam.

On a shelf was a decorative frame that still contained the picture it came with, a woman in a large-brimmed hat, laughing about something.

I got into Nicolas Cage's bed and called a bunch of girlfriends and said, "Guess where I am!"

Then I went to sleep.

I later found out that Mr. Cage's publicist was angry that I had mentioned the sleepover in the piece I wrote.

This seemed odd, because I thought it showed Mr. Cage to be a generous person.

And while I did snoop around, I had not mentioned anything even remotely embarrassing, like the shampoo in the bathroom, which was called Phytorhum for Lifeless Hair.

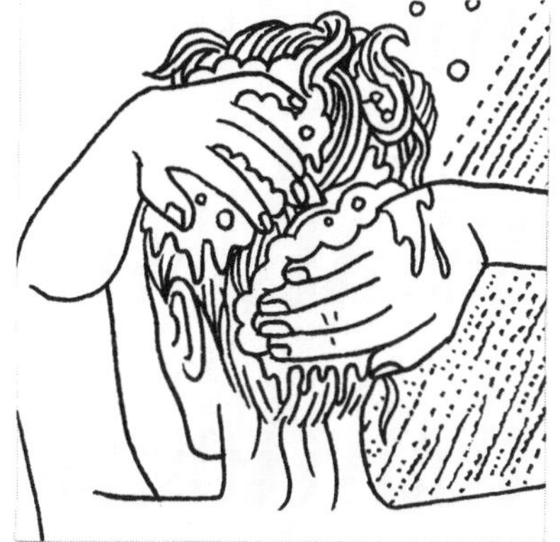

For all I knew that was Patricia Arquette's shampoo, or the shampoo that belonged to the last stupid reporter who missed her flight out because her car was locked in the parking lot.

ANDREW
SOLOMON

Notes on an Exorcism by Andrew Solomon

I'm not depressed now, but I lived with blinding depression for a long time.

Everything seemed hopeless and even getting out of bed was painful.

When I got better, I started researching various approaches to depression—treatments ranging from experimental brain surgery to hypnosis.

I wanted to explore the idea that there wasn't just one Western, modern, middle-class way of dealing with depressed people.

I wanted to show that it's a constant across class, culture, and history.

If you have brain cancer and decide that standing on your head and gargling for a half hour every day makes you feel better, it might make you feel better.

But you will likely still die from brain cancer.

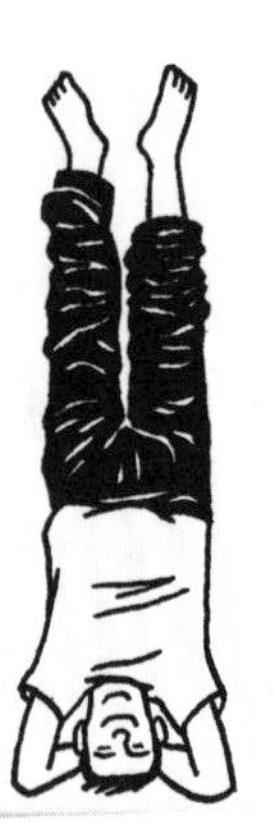

But if you suffer from depression and standing on your head and gargling for a half hour makes you feel better, then you are actually cured.

Because depression is an illness of how you feel.

This principle led me to search for cures of every kind in every place.

I visited my close friend David Hecht, then living in Senegal, who told me about the *ndeup*, a treatment for depression used by the Lebou people of West Africa.

David's then girlfriend, now ex-wife, Helene, had a cousin whose mother was a friend of someone who went to school with the daughter of a woman named Madame Diouf.

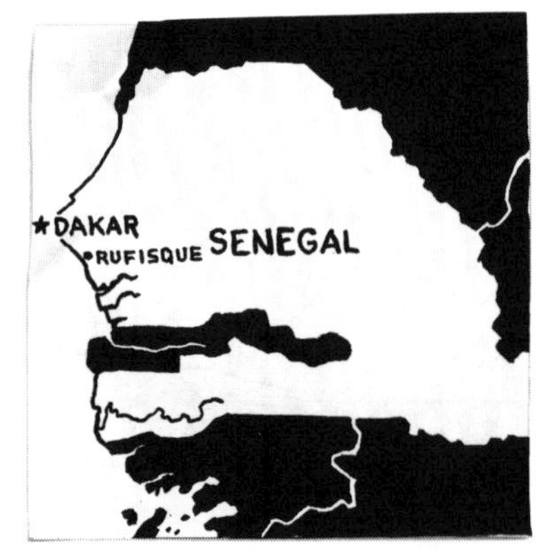

Madame Diouf lived two hours outside of Dakar in a town called Rufisque, and she practiced the *ndeup*. We decided to drop in.

She was an extraordinary old, large woman, wrapped in miles and miles of African fabric printed with images of eyes. I interviewed her about the *ndeup*.

Then I asked whether I could observe an *ndeup*, and she said that while she'd never had a foreigner, or *toubab*, do so before, she would allow me to, because I was a friend of Helene's.

I asked her when she thought she would next do one, and she said it would be sometime within six months. Since I didn't have six months to wait, I thanked her and turned to go.

It was at that moment that she said, "I hope you don't mind me saying this, but you don't look that great yourself."

I looked back at her doubtfully.

"I've certainly never done this for a *toubab* before," said Madame Diouf, "but I could do a *ndeup* for you."

"Well, yes," I said. "Sure," I said. "Yes, absolutely," I said. "Let's do that. I'll have a *ndeup*."

She gave me some fairly basic instructions and told me to come back in two days for the ceremony.

In the car, on the way back to Dakar, my translator, the aforementioned then girlfriend, now ex-wife of my friend, turned to me.

"Are you completely crazy? Do you have any idea what you're getting yourself into?"

"Well," I stammered, "being completely crazy is the whole idea; it's what got me here in the first place."

"I'll help you if you want," Helene said exasperatedly. "But you are totally crazy."

Madame Diouf had given us a shopping list of items to buy for the *ndeup*:

Seven yards of fabric.

A calabash.

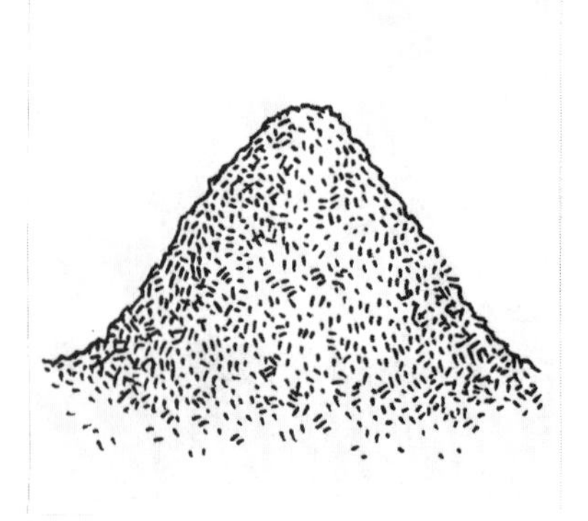

Seven kilos of millet.

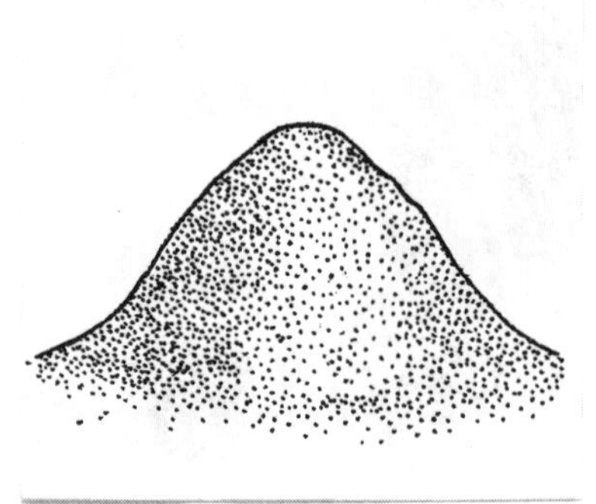

Five kilos of sugar.

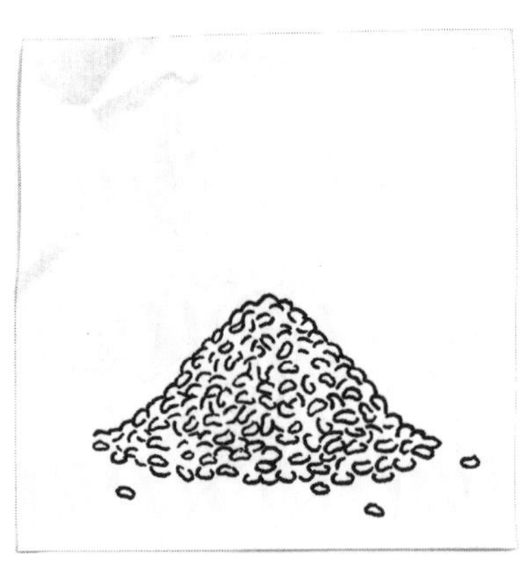

One kilo of cola beans.

Two cockerels.

And a ram.

Helene, David, and I went to market with a few other friends and bought all of the items, save one. "What about the ram?" I asked.

Sure enough, on the day of *ndeup*, as we drove to see Madame Diouf, we saw a shepherd by the side of the road. We pulled over and bought a ram for about seven dollars.

We struggled a bit to get the animal into the trunk of the taxi, but we did it. The driver didn't seem to mind that the ram kept relieving himself in the back of his car.

When we pulled into Rufisque around 8:00 a.m., I was feeling nervous.

Though I knew the rough idea, what actually happens in any *ndeup* varies enormously from person to person and depends on unpredictable messages from above.

To begin, I changed out of my jeans and T-shirt and put on a loincloth, and Madame Diouf and her attendants rubbed my chest and arms with the millet.

"We should really have music for this," said one of the attendants, disappearing into her home.

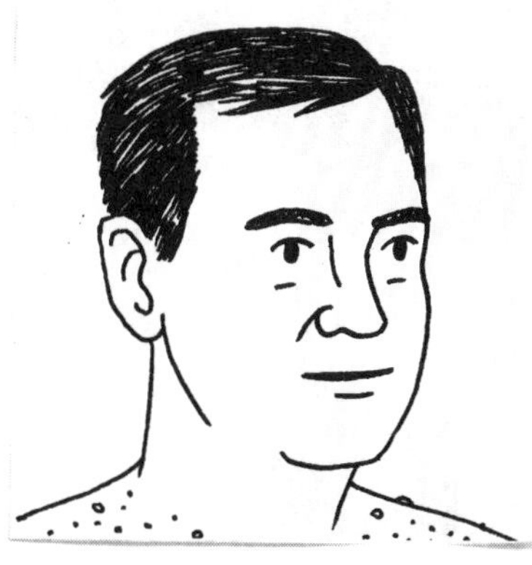

"Oh great!" I thought, expecting atmospheric drumming.

She returned, proudly holding her most prized possession, a battery-operated tape player, blaring music from the only tape she had, which was the soundtrack to *Chariots of Fire*.

I was given an assortment of sacred objects, which I held in my hands and feet and systematically dropped while Madame Diouf interpreted how each fell.

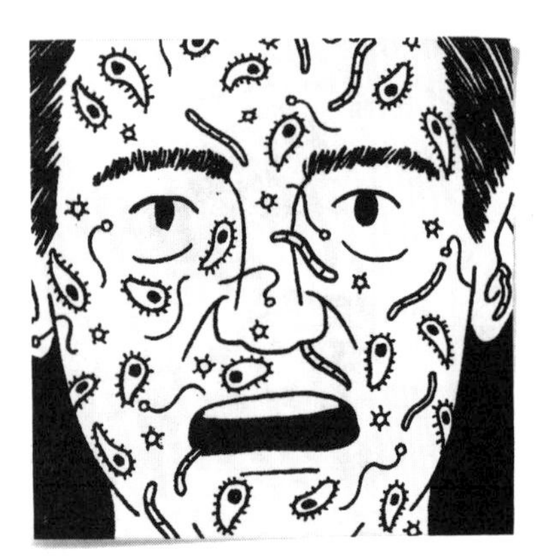
In Senegalese tradition, spirits are all over you—rather like microbes in the Western system—some good, some bad, some neutral.

Madame Diouf determined that I was haunted by jealous spirits who envied my real-life sexual partners, and that for my depression to be cured, these spirits would have to be mollified.

At that point the drumming began—wild, ecstatic drumming of the kind I'd been imagining all along.

I was led to the village's central square, where there was a small makeshift wedding bed that I got into with the ram.

I was told it would be very bad luck if the ram escaped, so I held on to him as tightly as I could, an arrangement that was clearly not making him happy.

The entire village had taken the day off from their work in the fields.

They danced around us in concentric circles, chanting loudly and throwing blankets and sheets of cloth over us.

We were gradually buried, and it was unbelievably hot and stifling under the heavy fabric, and the ram, who was having a very bad day, urinated all over my leg.

I couldn't see anything, but the sound of the drums and stamping feet grew more ecstatic and I was just about to pass out when suddenly all of the cloth was pulled off.

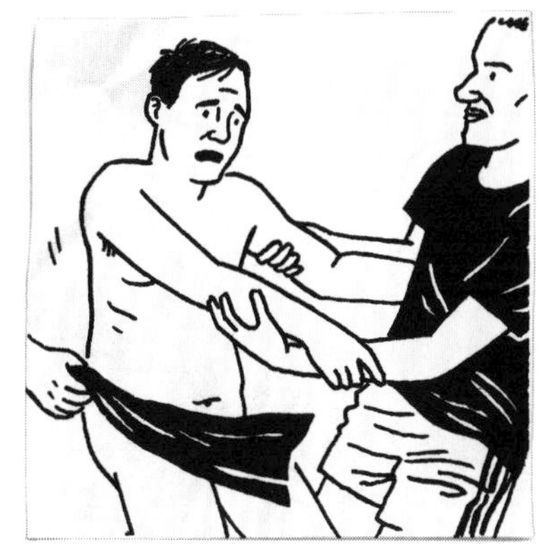

I was yanked to my feet and the loincloth was ripped from me.

The poor old ram's throat was slit, as were the throats of the two cockerels, and I was covered in their fresh blood.

So there I was, naked and totally covered in blood, and they said, "OK, that's the end of this part of it." Then we took a lunch break.

"Would you like a Coke?" asked one of Madame Diouf's attendants. I don't normally drink Coke, but at that moment it seemed like a really good idea.

I sat down, still naked, still covered in blood, surrounded by a swarm of interested flies, happily drinking a soda.

After I finished, the ram was hung from a nearby tree and butchered while a man used a long knife to dig several holes in the ground.

I was made to stand very straight with my hands by my sides and was then tied up with the ram's intestines.

Little bits of the ram's body were given to me and I shuffled around (which is really hard to do when you are tied up with intestines) and put the pieces into the holes.

All the while I had to say, "Spirits, leave me alone to complete the business of my life; know that I will never forget you."

Which struck me as a strangely touching and kind thing to say to the spirits I was exorcising.

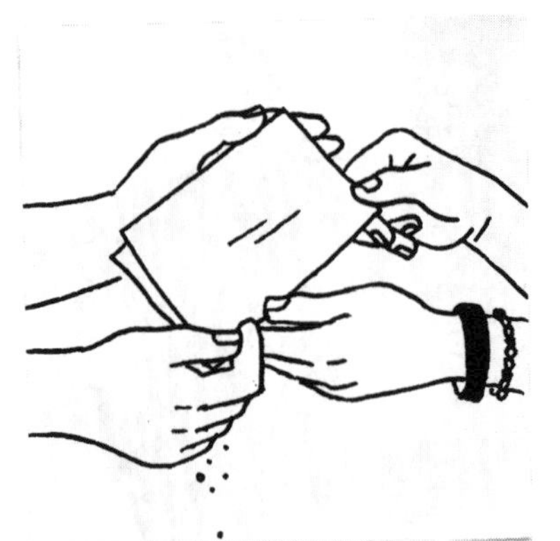

I was given a folded piece of paper in which all of the millet from the morning had been gathered.

I was instructed to sleep with it under my pillow and then in the morning give it to a beggar with good hearing and no deformities. Then all my troubles would end.

Then the women of the village filled their mouths with water and spit it out all over me, rinsing off the blood, much like a surround shower.

After I was clean, I changed back into my clothes and everyone danced and we barbecued the ram for dinner.

And I felt so up! Something in the day had made me feel so exhilarated, and it wasn't only the prospect of telling the story.

Five years later I was back in Africa and I had a conversation with a man in Rwanda about my *ndeup* experience.

"Oh, that's West Africa; this is East Africa," he said. "There are some similarities in our rituals, but things are quite different here."

"You know, we had a lot of trouble with Western mental-health workers who came to Rwanda after the genocide."

"What was the problem?" I asked.

"OK, their practice didn't involve being outside in the sun, which, as you experienced, is where you begin to feel better."

"There was no music or drumming to get your blood flowing."

"There was no sense of the entire community coming together to lift your spirits and bring you back to joy, as there was in your *ndeup*."

"Instead they took people, one at a time, into these dingy little rooms and had them sit there for an hour and talk about bad things that had happened to them."

"Of course, it made the depressed people feel worse."

"We had to ask these health workers to leave the country."

HANNAH
TINTI

The First Time I Almost Died by Hannah Tinti

When I was five years old, I went to a kindergarten that was in the basement of a church. For recess, we would play in the graveyard.

It was an old graveyard, with stones from the 1600s and 1700s. Some people said it was haunted.

But I'd never seen any ghosts there.

The stones were black slate or sandstone or granite. They tipped left and right, and some were broken.

They had strange faces on them, and trees and angel wings. I thought they were beautiful.

My friends and I played house behind a stone wall that marked off a family plot.

I was wearing a thick Irish sweater, and I took it off and hung it on one of the graves, as if it was a coat rack.

We shared a dinner of twigs and leaves.

Then we all went to sleep. We pretended the headstones were the headboards of our beds. We stretched in front of them on the grass.

I thought about the real family buried beneath us. I wondered how far down their bodies were.

One of the teachers rang the bell to go back inside.

I hurried to get my sweater, and on my way something reached out and tripped me.

I collapsed onto one of the broken gravestones, and a jagged piece of slate went through my left wrist.

I didn't understand what had happened. I lifted my head from the ground. And then I saw blood. Lots of it.

One of the teachers grabbed me and started to run.

She ran all over the school, screaming, with me hanging over her shoulder.

Her shirt was splashed with red.

I found out later that I had severed the artery.

Two cops came and rushed me to the hospital in their squad car, with the sirens on.

My teacher sat with me in the backseat, squeezing my wrist behind the cage, and I watched everyone pull over for us.

My room at the hospital had a painting of Snow White and the seven dwarfs on the wall.

Dopey and Doc were the only ones recognizable; the rest looked sinister and strangely alike.

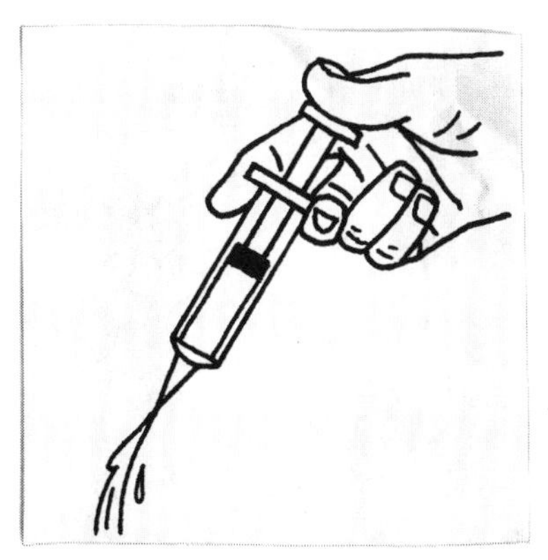

One of the nurses had a big plastic plunger. She filled it with ice water and then squirted the ice water into my open wrist.

It hurt. I screamed. It took five nurses to hold me down on the table.

One was on my legs, one was on my right arm, one was holding my head, and two were holding down my wrist.

My parents were at a Red Sox game. This was in 1978—no cell phones.

Every once in a while, one of the nurses would stick her head into the room and say my parents were on their way.

But they never came.

A doctor walked in. He had a small round mirror strapped to his head. He was friendly.

Then I kicked him in the face, and he wasn't so friendly anymore.

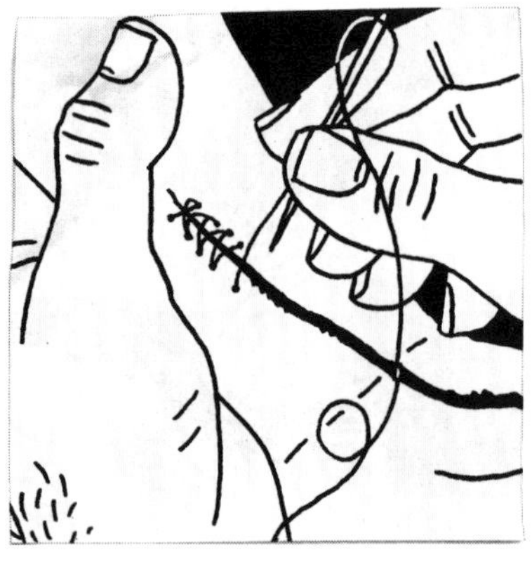

He took out all the pieces of the grave from inside me and then he started sewing.

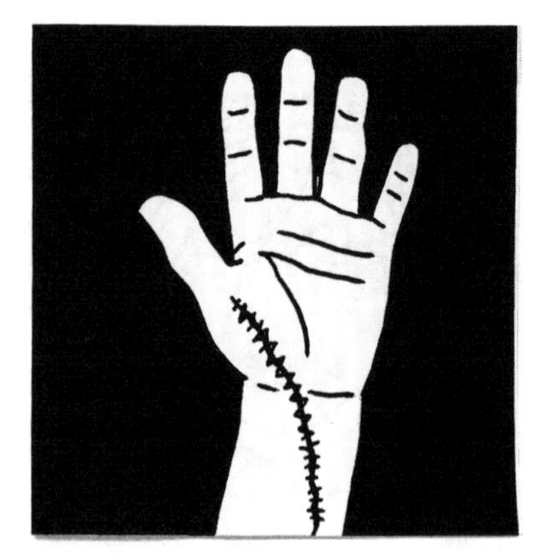

It felt like he was going to sew my whole arm up.

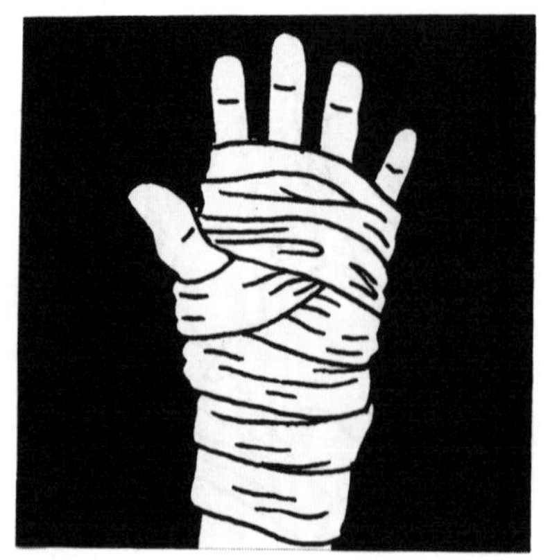

The nurses wrapped my wrist in rolls of white bandages.

When they were finished, one of them gave me the plastic plunger.

My teacher brought me to her apartment and put me on a couch with a blanket.

My hand swelled up and I couldn't bend my fingers.

She made me a cup of tea. I couldn't drink it.

I felt like I'd aged a century.

Like I'd traded bones with one of the bodies in the graveyard.

I waited on the couch all afternoon, until the Red Sox game was over, and my parents went to pick me up from kindergarten, found out what had happened, and came to take me home.

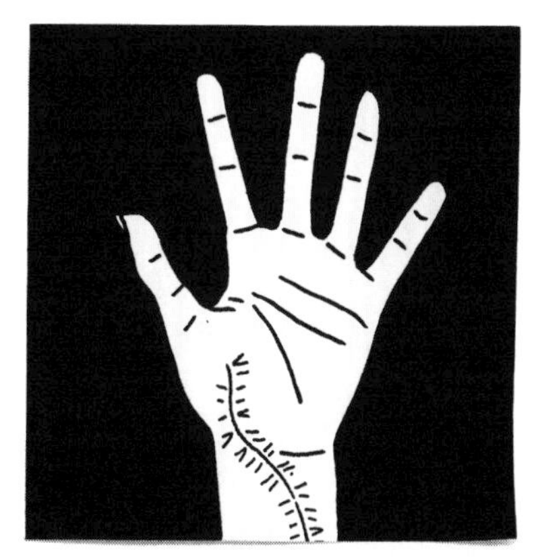

My left hand ended up being fine—only some nerve damage, so I can't put my middle finger and ring finger together.

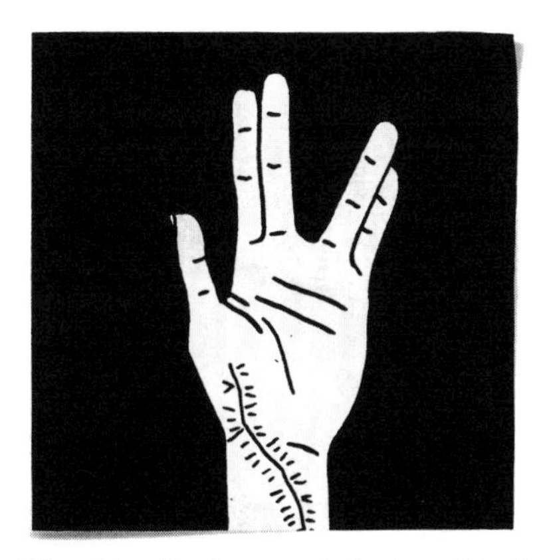

When I try, the fingers get stuck and I look like I'm delivering the "live long and prosper" salute from *Star Trek*.

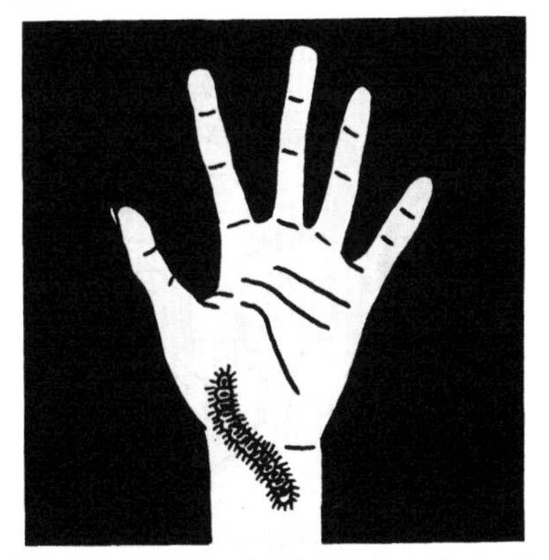

There's also a scar that twists from the heel of my hand down past the tendons and blue veins. It looks like a centipede trapped under the surface.

The marks from the stitches fan out in all directions. And the skin there always feels tight.

A few years ago, I went back to the cemetery where it had happened, and took some pictures. It felt like walking into a dream—everything was out of perspective.

The family plot where we used to play was a tiny stone wall that only came up to my knees.

There was a bump in the middle of the yard that I remembered being an enormous hill. The whole place was different, but also the same.

I tried to find the grave where I had fallen. I was curious to see whose name had gone into my body. But the broken stones were unreadable, just piles of slate.

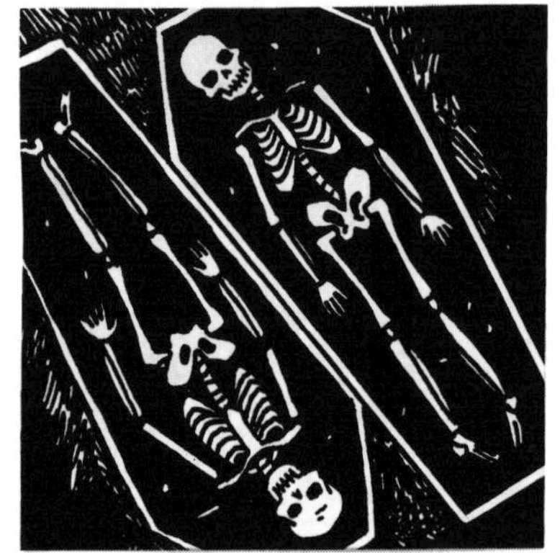

There was no way to know who was there under the ground. Hundreds of years had passed since anyone who remembered them had lived.

The bodies were still there, though. I could sense them when I crossed over.

And the stones were still beautiful.

MARIE
LORENZ

Shipwrecked
by Marie Lorenz

I have an art project called the *Tide and Current Taxi*, in which I ferry people around New York City in a boat I made.

I call the boat a taxi because I'd like for people to use it as an alternative means of transportation around the city.

I call it an art project because I rarely get people where they actually want to go.

Manhattan is an island, situated in a huge tidal estuary, and even the distant boroughs are connected by a system of rivers, creeks, canals, bays, and inlets.

For example, you can push off from a boardwalk in Staten Island and float across the Lower New York Bay to Swinburne Island, where you can see migrating harbor seals resting on their way to Nova Scotia.

You can also paddle from a pier in Harlem, cruise for a mile along shallow Dutch Kills Creek, and dock on quiet North Brother Island.

North Brother is now a bird sanctuary, but on it sit the ruins of an abandoned hospital that was used to quarantine New York's most contagious and criminal patients.

The small house where Typhoid Mary was imprisoned in 1915 is still there, forgotten and rotting away.

When I moved to New York in 2005 I started sailing to these sorts of "secret" places and became fascinated by the strength of the current in the harbor.

It seemed possible that with a little planning and an understanding of tidal charts you could simply hop in a boat and ride the current wherever you needed to go.

I've been building boats for years. My earliest efforts were in art school—simple dinghies made out of scrap plywood.

Over the years, my skills have developed and my boats have become more elaborate.

But for the taxi I wanted to build something simple, light, and durable. So I made a plywood double-ender, fourteen feet long and slightly wider than a canoe.

Sturdy yet buoyant. Pretty yet practical. Just like New York City itself.

With my plywood taxi complete, all I needed was a passenger and a destination.

I sent an e-mail solicitation to everyone I knew. The message got passed around and I eventually heard from a friend of a friend of friend, named Joe Potts.

Joe wanted to take my taxi from Williamsburg to Manhattan—a quick commute across the East River, perfect for my project's maiden voyage.

I met Joe a week later with my boat on an abandoned beach near North Sixth Street in Brooklyn.

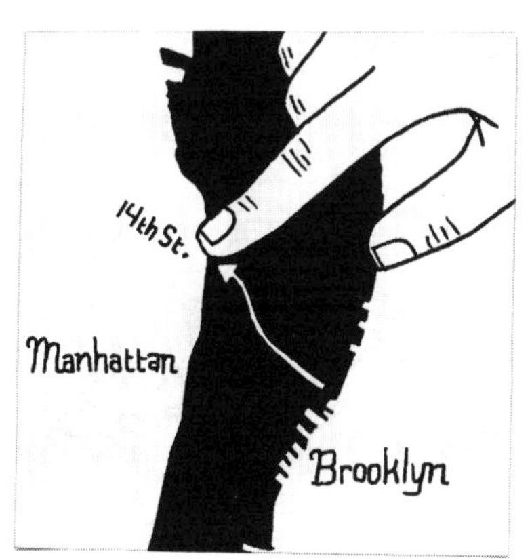

The current was flowing northward, so I proposed floating along the Brooklyn coast until we were parallel to Fourteenth Street in Manhattan.

At which point we could paddle across the river, dock, and grab some coffee.

Joe took a seat in the bow of the boat, I took one in the stern, and off we went.

The tide did carry us north as planned, but the wind pushed us much faster than I'd anticipated.

Before I knew it we were parallel with the United Nations building, swept a good thirty blocks north of Fourteenth.

We made our break for Manhattan just past Roosevelt Island, a strip of land between Manhattan and Queens just a few blocks north of the UN.

As we crossed, we found ourselves in the path of ferries and tour boats pulling in and out of a high-traffic dock nearby.

In open water it's not that difficult to pilot a small boat through the wake of a big one: You sort of paddle in at an angle and let the waves roll under you.

But this wasn't open water, and as we neared Manhattan we got into some trouble near a steep iron seawall.

The wake from the larger boats ricocheted off the taxi in steep triangular waves that were impossible for us to ride through.

Soon water was violently crashing over both sides of our boat.

"Worst-case scenario," Joe yelled to me, "we flag down another boat to help us, right?"

"Joe," I said, "this *is* the worst-case scenario."

We paddled as hard as we could away from the seawall and back toward Roosevelt Island while the boat's hull rapidly filled with water.

We tried to bail out the water but it was no use.

At some point the boat just sort of disappeared from under us and we found ourselves swimming in the East River's shipping lane.

Huge boats were bearing down on us from the north and south, oblivious to our struggle.

As we swam, I tried to keep my mouth shut. The water was warm and salty and smelled like a sewer.

We were five hundred feet from Roosevelt Island but the tide was pulling us north, away from the shore, toward Hell Gate, an infamous tidal strait known for swallowing boats whole.

The boat had capsized; I tried to tow it behind me as I swam but the pull from Hell Gate was too strong.

I was exhausted from paddling and weighed down by my clothes and shoes. Somewhere around the Fifty-ninth Street bridge, Joe convinced me to let go of the boat.

As it drifted away my heart sank. The prettiest boat I had ever made—an entire summer's worth of work—down the drain.

Free of the boat, we swam to Roosevelt Island and dragged ourselves up the rocky embankment.

As we sorted through our stuff—dead camera, dead cell phone, wet wallet—we started to laugh. The situation was incredible.

There we were, shipwrecked and stranded on an island—all within a mile of Times Square.

As we walked toward the Roosevelt Island subway stop, I caught sight of the boat floating upside down in a tangle of gear.

The tide was still pushing her north, but she seemed to be matching our pace, almost lingering alongside us.

I couldn't abandon her.

I kicked off my shoes, tore off my life jacket, and dove back into the toxic, smelly river.

It was much easier to swim without my shoes or life jacket and I was able to haul the mess back to shore pretty easily.

But now that I had my boat back, I had to ask myself: What was I going to do with it?

I'd been a terrible sailor and had put a stranger at risk. The answer was clear.

My taxi service was over after one lousy trip.

Later that night, back in Brooklyn, I sat down at my computer to send out a mass e-mail telling all my friends and potential passengers about the demise of my project.

But before I hit Send, I got an e-mail from Joe's roommate. Joe had told her about the shipwreck, and how we almost got cut in half by a tour boat and nearly drowned in the East River.

He'd also said it was the most fun he'd ever had in New York.

"I'd love to come along on the next trip," she wrote. "And I can swim."

DAVID
REES

Three Gorges Goddamn
by David Rees

China is one of the top ten most important countries in the world. If you don't believe that, you don't know what century you're living in. I should know; I've been to China.

I visited China with my three best friends from high school, Aaron, Jon, and Mike.

Everyone has that one friend who's always ahead of the curve, the one who was into Led Zeppelin before anyone else, like back in 1953.

"*Saturday Night Live*? Sure, it used to be funny—*back when I watched it, back in 1844.*"

That's what my friend Aaron was like with China. He was into China *way* before anyone else.

By the time writers like Thomas Friedman first started running around screaming, "China! China!"

Aaron could already go into a Chinese restaurant in China and order Chinese food in Chinese.

So Aaron invited Jon and Mike and me to visit him in Toledo, Ohio.

Just kidding! He invited us to visit him in Nanjing, China.

As you know, all your high school friends have crazy obsessions.

Aaron's obsession is China, obviously, because why else would you live there?

Jon's obsession is urban infrastructure. He calls it "infra" for short.

So he agreed to visit China because it's on a total infra binge right now, building suspension bridges over highways inside skyscrapers under overpasses.

Mike's obsession is international travel. So he agreed to visit China because what's more international than that?

And me? I'm obsessed with my high school friends. Why? Because they're effortlessly cool and funny. I don't know how they do it. It's hard to describe.

But I feel like a beached whale made entirely of thumbs when I'm around them—one who can't stop cracking up. So I agreed to visit China because that's where my friends would be.

As you know, all your high school friends have superpowers.

Aaron's superpower is China.

Jon's superpower is the ability to interpret everything in the universe through the lens of our home state North Carolina's demography.

(We're talking about a guy who has a four-foot-tall stack of almanacs.)

Example: Aaron was explaining something about the Chinese city of Yichang, and Jon cut in:

"I get it. Yichang is like the Goldsboro of China."

(I know so little about demography, it took me a while to realize that the Goldsboro of North Carolina is Goldsboro, North Carolina.)

Mike's superpower is overpreparation. He prepared for the trip by printing out information on everything, including a list of the tallest buildings in the world, some of which are in China.

"Dude, we are *so* visiting the Jin Mao Tower! That thing is totally badass. Thirteen hundred eighty feet."

My superpower is being a curmudgeon. I prepared for the trip by buying a new pair of comfortable shoes.

Because I knew that if you wore sneakers abroad, the locals would mark you as a loathsome American dork.

"Guys, if you want to blend in, don't wear sneakers. It's probably like France."

Guess what? If you're a gangly white American in China, it doesn't matter what shoes you wear—not even if they're coal-burning plastic sandals with Mao's face on them—you won't blend in.

Anyway, one fine day the four of us exploited our superpowers (and our credit cards) and rendezvoused in China.

We decided to build our trip around a visit to the infamous, headline-gobbling Three Gorges Dam, one of the largest specimens of infra on earth.

You know about this dam, right? The one that cost twenty-six billion dollars? The one with thirty-two generators, each of which weighs six thousand tons?

The one that's supposed to generate one hundred thousand gigawatt hours per year?

The one that required the displacement of more than a million people?

Mao's great dark dream, finally brought to fruition.

To pay our respects to the dam, we needed to take a boat trip up the Yangtze River. But what kind of boat would we take?

Would we take the expensive boat and travel in comfort among other Westerners and basically sell out like a bunch of richie-rich kids?

Or would we take the modest, authentic Chinese boat that all the Chinese people took, the boat that cost less than a bicycle ride?

Democracy rules in China, so we voted on which boat to take. Not wanting to be confused with Western dandies, we voted for authenticity and economy.

Before the boat even left the dock I regretted our decision. It was crowded and filthy and our cabin was so small it made my freshman dorm room seem like the Biltmore Estate.

The ceilings were so low I had to walk around like a hunchback and I kept conking my head.

My theory is that the boat folks kept the ticket price so low by installing the boat's engine backward.

It seemed as if diesel fumes were being sucked out of the smog-filled air and into the boat. It was like a film running in reverse.

We voted again. Should we leave the bad-news boat while we still could? All but one of us voted to stay on the boat. Hooray for democracy! Anchors aweigh!

We spent our first day on the boat, on deck, taking in the pollution and posing for Chinese families' photographs.

They positioned us on the bow of the ship like Leonardo DiCaprio in *Titanic*. This was actually very fun.

If we had been on the Western tourist boat, I doubt anyone would've posed us like Leonardo DiCaprio and taken our photo while giggling.

The rest of the time was spent sweating and bumping into things and sitting in our tiny cabin.

The cabin had a television and we had smuggled a bizarre off-brand video-game console onboard with us.

But one of us knocked over the television and broke it, so we couldn't even play *Submarine-Arthritis Baseball Fight*, or whatever it was.

A couple of days into the boat trip we had a second argument about whether to bail.

We were snapping at one another and one of us named Mike might have even raised his voice at one of us named David.

And that's not cool—not even on a boat that is floating over the dynamited ruins of flooded villages and shattered lives.

It was a tense afternoon. Then we arrived at the Three Gorges Dam. We grabbed our cameras and boarded a bus to take a closer look.

The Three Gorges Dam is really big. It's one of those things that is so big, you lose track of how big it is.

It starts to look small, and right as you're thinking, "What's the big deal? It isn't so big," you notice that a big tour bus looks as tiny as an ant's butthole beside it.

Needless to say, the Chinese tourists were really excited about it.

It's the biggest thing they've built since the Great Wall.

And, truth be told, if America had built this thing, it'd be on the one-dollar bill already.

But the dam made me depressed. When it breaks (and it's totally gonna break; engineers are already sounding the alarm), millions of people living in cities downriver will die.

Could the pride of China also be . . . its downfall?

Just kidding—China's not having a downfall anytime soon. The twenty-first century belongs to China. As does the next century. And the next.

Basically, by the time we reach the end of China's reign, the Earth will be a smoldering asteroid of nuclear goo floating in an interstellar oil slick, so it won't really matter. (Sorry, India.)

We returned to the boat feeling exhausted and unhappy.

Later that evening Aaron and I called an emergency meeting for us all to talk about our feelings about one another.

I'm not going to say that Jon and Mike are scared of talking about feelings . . . but they literally ran away.

They literally ran away *inside a boat.*

We didn't see Jon and Mike for a while. Were they hiding in strangers' cabins?

Were they down in the engine room, making sure the engine had enough coal and old newspapers and uranium to keep belching smoke everywhere?

Is there an analogy to be made between Jon and Mike's refusal to express their feelings and a huge dam straining against the weight of backed-up water, putting innocent lives at risk?

That's not for me to say. But if it were, I'd definitely have a few things to say about it.

Finally we were all so claustrophobic and miserable and tired of my complaining that Aaron convinced the captain to pull over in the dead of night to let us off.

We slipped off the boat while the rest of the passengers slept, without saying good-bye.

I like to imagine that the Chinese passengers remember us as four Leonardo DiCaprio–shaped phantoms who wouldn't stop bickering.

"Remember when we went to see the Three Gorges Dam? Remember those Americans who were arguing and bumping their heads the whole time?"

"Do you think they fell into the Yangtze River? I hope they're OK."

JEFF
SIMMERMON

Big Black Bird
by Jeff Simmermon

I kind of had cancer last summer, for a little bit. At first, the only sign was that I'd been moving much more slowly than usual during Muay Thai training.

I was having trouble getting the pads to the right place in time to catch my sparring partner's kicks. I thought it was because I was pretty sleep deprived and stressed out at work.

Then, during a sparring session, this little Dominican guy a foot shorter than I am kicked me square in the nuts and I nearly passed out.

I went home, and then to the doctor, where we discovered a tumor roughly the size and density of a Cadbury egg growing in the center of my left testicle.

"This has got to come out soon," the doctor said.

"How soon?"

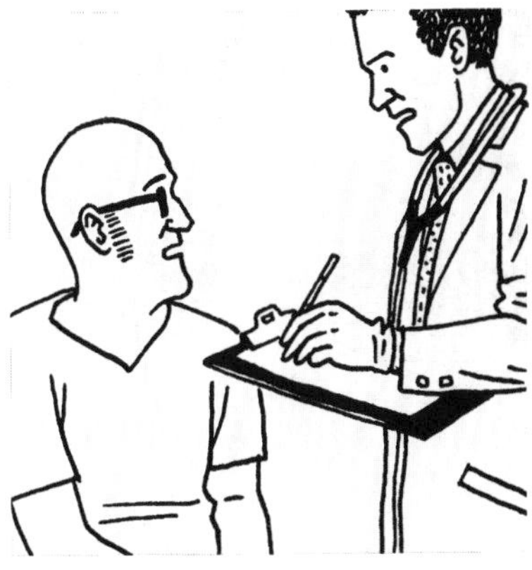

"Tomorrow."

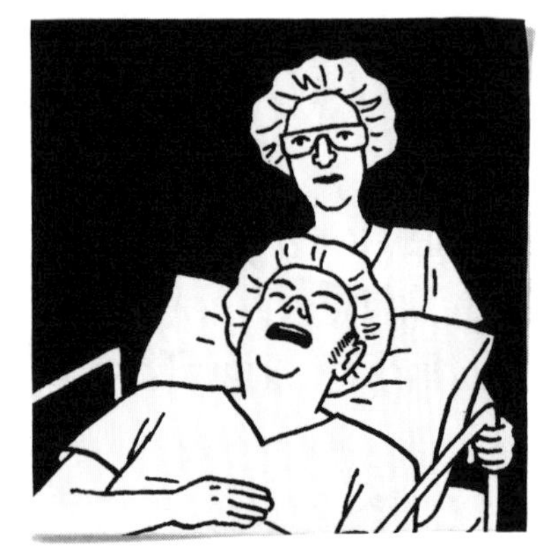

When I had my tonsils removed I was drugged into submission in another room and wheeled into surgery.

This time, it was very important to the doctor that I walk into the operating room under my own power. I don't think I'll ever understand why.

It felt like walking into my own autopsy in the belly of a flying saucer.

Surgical white light blazed off the tips of every shining scalpel and beamed hot right on my brain's fight-or-flight reflex.

Everyone in the room was garbed up for surgery in the same mask, gloves, and robe.

I stood there in the room, freezing in the sterile air, trying very hard not to run.

Suddenly all the doctors turned to look at me simultaneously, like aliens pretending to care. One of the taller ones said in a cool, flat tone, "Welcome, Mister Simmermon."

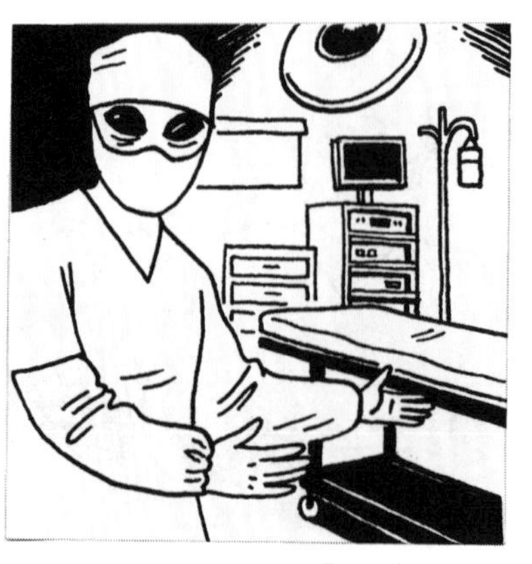

"We've been expecting you. Everything is going to be fine. Just get up onto this table and relax."

The corona of light beyond the surgical lamps faded fast to a deep-space blackness.

The blackness took the shape of a large bird. The black bird rose up and spread its wings, folding me into a void between its wings and carrying me deep into the mother ship.

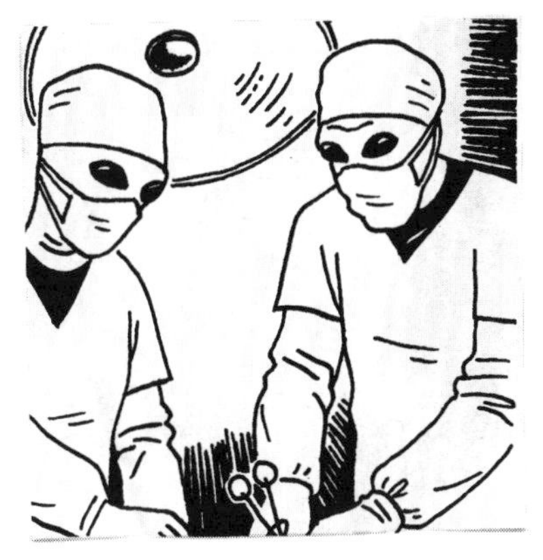

They cut all the cancer out by simply removing my left testicle. No more surgery, no chemo, no radiation. I should have felt lucky, and I did, sort of.

I'd only had cancer for a short time, and it was over.

As I was lying in bed at home that first night after surgery, the big black bird from the hospital fluttered down and landed on my chest.

It crept up my torso and balanced its icy claws on my throat, then tilted its beak into my ear and began to whisper.

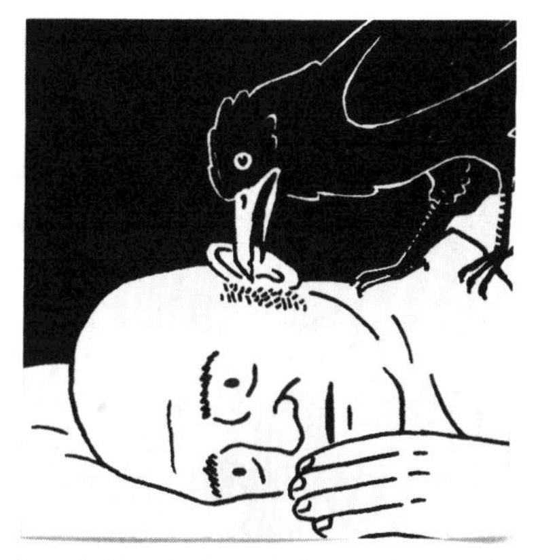

It said, "Your body might be healthy now, but things are going to be different from here on. People are going to find it really, really hard to relate to you."

"Nobody's going to understand you. So go easy on yourself. You're never going to stop needing people, but eventually you'll get used to feeling all alone."

Family and friends circled around me and showered me with love and affection. My mother came and stayed with me for a week, and I got to be her child all over again for a little while.

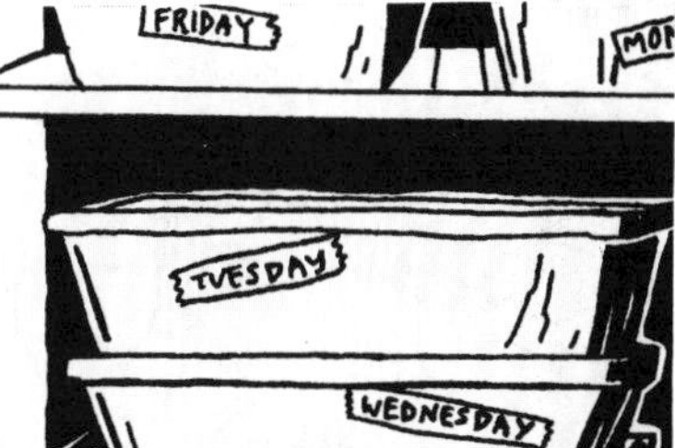

My coworkers sent us a week's worth of free meals so we could focus on spending time together.

And my girlfriend decided to move up to New York from Washington just to live closer to me.

And beyond that, I discovered so many beautiful, wonderful people who had been right next to me all along, quietly at the periphery of my life.

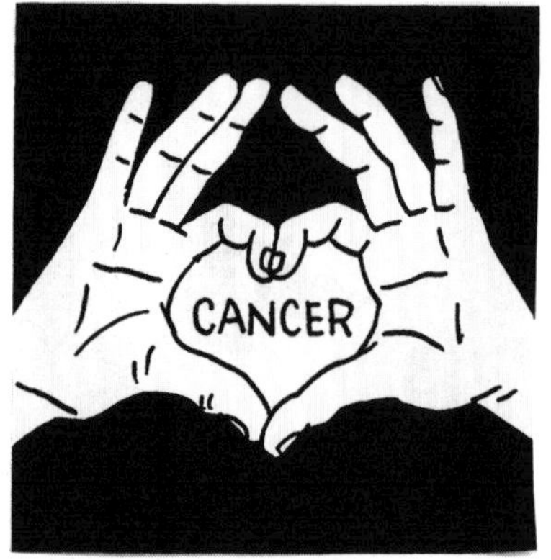

If you're feeling lonely or unloved, I can't recommend cancer enough. It really gives you the boost that you're looking for—in the short term, at least.

The support was amazing, but eventually I found its limits. There was only so much these people could understand; nobody else had suddenly lost a testicle or any other body part.

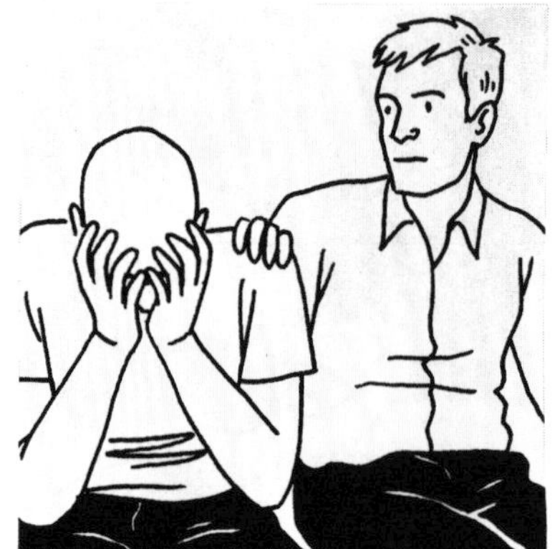

I told my best friend, "Dude, I am so depressed right now."

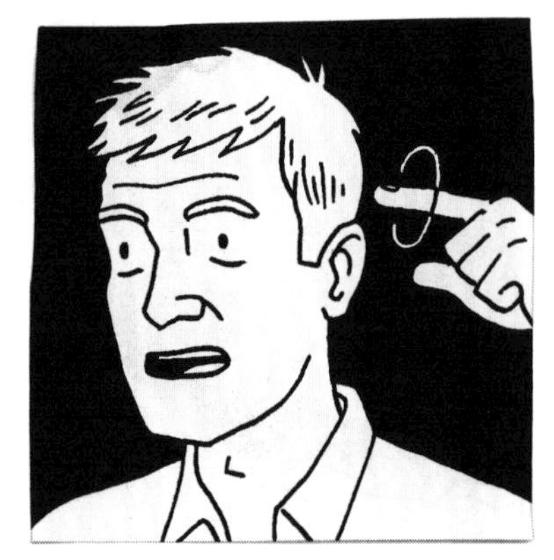

"Well, good," he said. "You just got one of your balls cut off. If you're not depressed, you're crazy."

Once my body healed, I returned to work, started going back to the gym and doing all the things that I'd done before I got sick.

I felt like the last man dancing after somebody unplugs the jukebox and turns out the lights.

I looked perfectly healthy. People came up to me and said, "You're looking great, man, looking real great! How are you feeling?" There was no right answer to that question.

You really don't want to tell someone, "I feel like an android that has been programmed to act just like me."

I felt like a photocopy of a photocopy, conveying the essential information but blurred and distorted, fading away at the edges.

The bird came to visit me every night, as soon as I was in bed and alone. One night it said, "You've lost your passion, man. You used to be so vital and full of energy."

"Now this weird Jungian thing happened to you and it's like you got stripped of something invisible. And you can't even be bothered to mourn the loss."

"I know, you're so right," I said. "It's like I've been half-neutered." "Well, you have," the bird replied. "And it's not coming back, either."

I asked my nurse at Sloan-Kettering if they had a support group for this sort of thing. The nurse said, "It's funny, we really don't."

"The best cancer center on earth and you guys can't get some folding chairs and shitty coffee together? You sure about this?" "We tried, but nobody came."

"This kind of cancer mostly affects young guys, and we find that they really don't want to talk about it. You might get some value out of a different support group, though. Maybe you could—"

"What," I interrupted, "take over a brain cancer one and make it all about me?"

Sometimes I would see children with cancer in the waiting room when I went to get a CT scan.

I'd see them sitting there, so small and gray and submitting so bravely to their fate, and my heart would drift even lower.

I was so physically healthy and these kids weren't ever going to drive. Poor me.

Recursive self-abuse; there's nothing quite like it—beating yourself up for beating yourself up.

When you get a CT scan, you have to arrive an hour early in order to marinate your body tissues in a pink liquid.

It tastes exactly like robot piss sweetened with antifreeze.

During one of my many trips, I was sitting in the waiting room sipping a bottle of this sweet secretion when I noticed an Indian couple across the room.

The woman was completely bald, and I am fairly certain she'd had a double mastectomy.

She crossed her legs into a prayer pose and began to meditate. Her husband moved to give her some space and sat down next to me.

Shortly after a nurse took the woman away, her husband elbowed me and said, "So, what are you in for?"

I told him, and he winced. Every guy does it, every time.

Then he said, "You know, in my religion, we believe in destiny. We believe that things happen to you for reasons you may not understand."

"They just happen and you choose the way in which you adjust. Given that, I'd say my wife's cancer hasn't been an entirely bad thing."

"In twenty-seven years of marriage there are ups and there are downs, and when she got diagnosed, we were on a down."

"Now we are communicating better, and we're closer with each other and our children. Our grown children—who have left the house and are not even Hindu anymore—we are closer than ever."

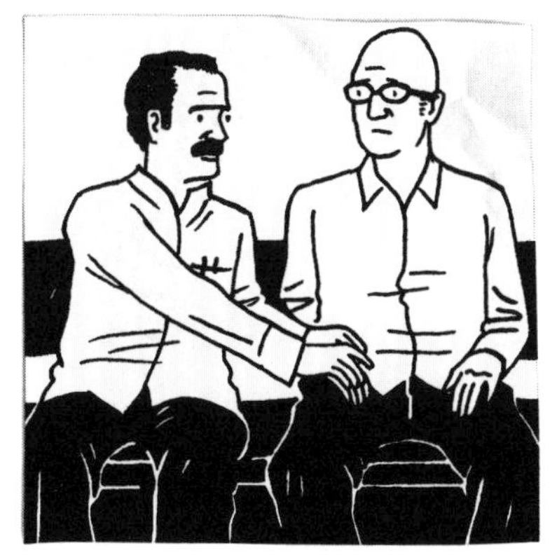

He turned to me and clasped my hand tightly with both of his, then looked me right in the eyes."Something good is going to come of this," he said. "You're young and strong and you' re going to live.

"And all you have to do is find it, then allow it into your heart. And once you let that thing into your heart, you will really know what it is to live."

For the first time since my diagnosis, and probably much longer than that, I was able to cry, let it all out, all that pent-up emotion after months of being strong for everyone but myself.

Then the nurse took me away and the guy looked at me and gave me two huge thumbs up, his mustache stretched wide over a tremendous toothy grin.

I see him all the time, pretty much every night when the big black bird shows up.

If I close my eyes and concentrate very hard, I can conjure his Cheshire mustache, hovering over that big black bird on my chest.

One day I'm going to believe him, and that big black bird is just going to fly away.

DAVID
RAKOFF
SHEA STA
U
D

All Together Now
by David Rakoff

"You guys have concussions," the coordinator says to the two little boys, ages five and seven.

"What's that?" the older one asks.

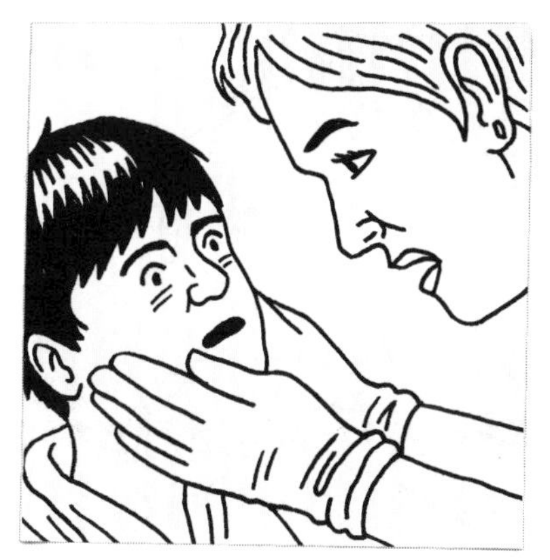

"It's a bad knock to the head. It means riding in the ambulance," she says, her hand on his sweet cheek, her brows knit in concern.

"Ambulaaaaance!" the boys yell, fists raised above their heads in joyous triumph, their faces radiating delight, their fondest dreams realized.

The burns on my legs are relatively minor.

I took the brunt of the blast to my upper body. My forearms are so severely burned that the bones are visible in places.

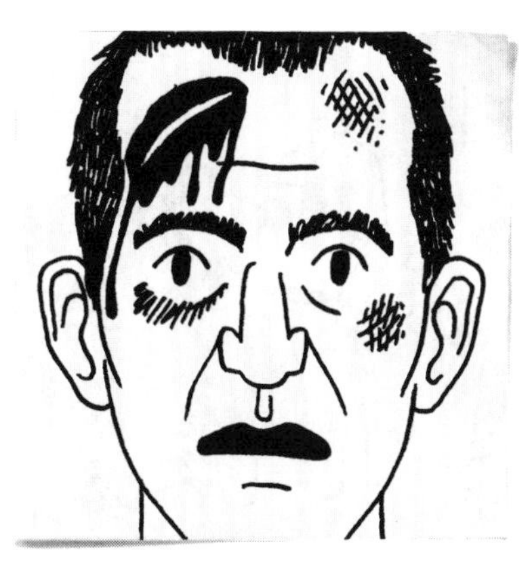

Lesser damage is to my face—some lacerations from flying debris on my cheeks and forehead, but I can walk just fine.

Most important, my eyes escaped damage. I must have held my hands up in front of my face in an automatic gesture of self-protection in the split second when the explosion happened.

"You want the rest of my Lorna Doones?" asks the woman seated beside me. She has managed only half of one in the four-pack we have each been given.

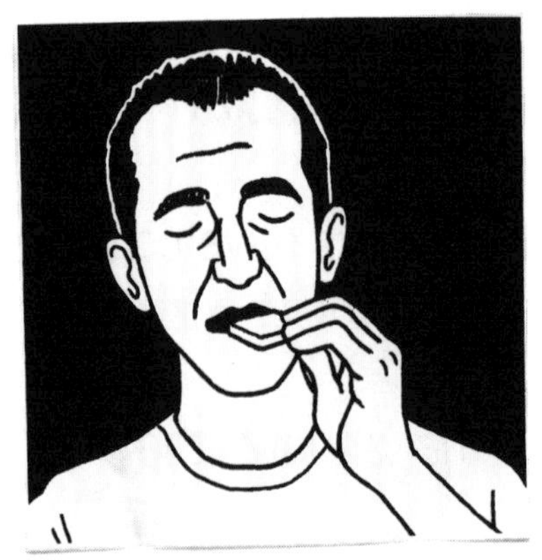
Trauma clearly makes me hungry, because I tore through mine in less than a minute.

I look over her information tag and ask if her dislocated shoulder and fractured ankle have put her off her food.

"No, I had that gastric bypass surgery so I can only have a little taste of something and then I'm full. I lost a hundred and twenty pounds so far."

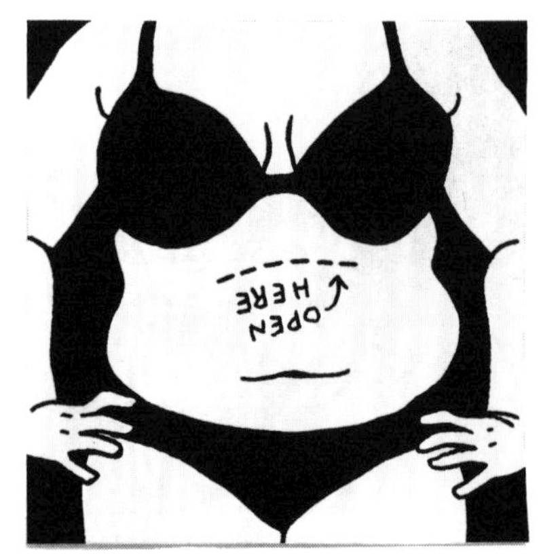

"The day of my operation I drew a zipper on my stomach with a Sharpie and wrote 'Open Here.' I like to joke and get 'em in a good mood before surgery."

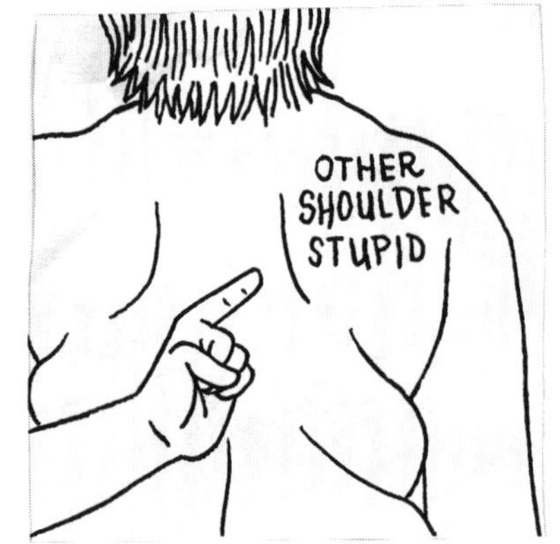

"I wrote 'Other shoulder, stupid' when I had my rotator cuff sewn up."

"If there's one thing you need to know about me," she says, as though preparing me for our long future together, "it's that I joke around *a lot*."

There are about twenty of us here this Sunday morning, mostly Bellevue employees and their kids.

We have been corralled up to the fourteenth-floor cafeteria to wait for Operation United Response to begin.

Sponsored by the Office of Homeland Security, it is a citywide, interagency simulation drill.

Today's exercise will work through the logistics of how law enforcement, intelligence, paramedics, and hospitals would respond to the detonation of a dirty bomb at Shea Stadium.

I signed up to be a victim.

We all wear our symptoms around our necks, laminated cards on chains giving our gender, our age (I have jumped half a decade and am forty-five years old on this day), and what is wrong with us.

The cards are for our reference only; the people treating us—EMTs and hospital staff—will be responding only to the symptoms we display.

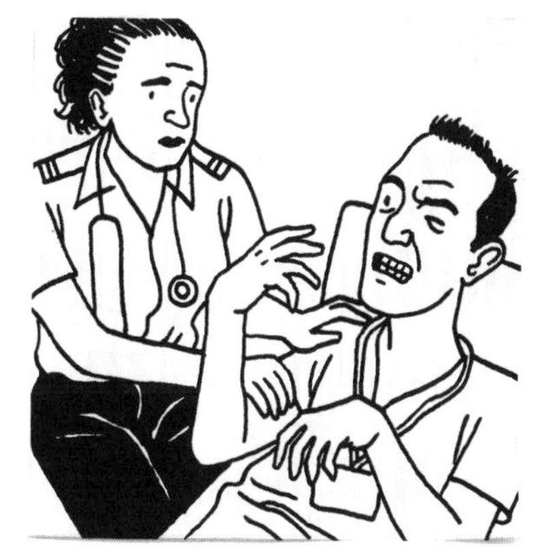

For this reason, our instruction sheets tell us never to stop acting at any point during the four hours that OUR lasts.

We are also admonished against overacting, and strictly prohibited from milking any extra on-site sympathy or drama by ad-libbing symptoms.

Finally, if we feel unwell at any point, or if we're unwilling to continue for any reason, we need only utter the safe word *code red* and we will be released.

Nobody knew what the disaster was going to be beforehand. The hospital was just as in the dark as the victims, which makes sense if you're testing for spur-of-the-moment preparedness.

I was told one thing only: Be prepared to get wet, in case the scenario demanded a decontamination shower. So I am wearing my bathing suit under my clothes.

We are taken downstairs and put into oversize blue paper scrubs.

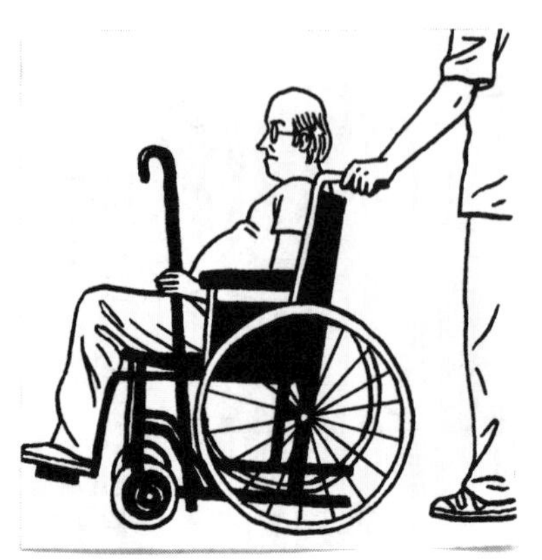

The less ambulatory of us are spirited off somewhere.

My group is the walking wounded, who could presumably have made it to the hospital under our own power. (But how? I wonder.)

Shea Stadium is out in Flushing, and although I can walk, remember that the bones of my forearms are showing through my burned flesh. Did I take the subway?

(Even with these injuries, would I have been the worst-looking person on the train?)

We are taken out back to the driveway near the emergency entrance.

We stand on the curb, careful not to block the path of any oncoming vehicle, although there isn't one in sight on this quiet Sunday. It is the middle of March. Spring has barely begun.

The bark on the bare trees is starting to blacken with moisture, and a few branches are sporting vivid lime green buds.

We are a group of five, our oldest and youngest simultaneously housed in a fifteen-year-old girl playing a grandmother.

For now, though, we're just being ourselves as we stand around for half an hour without seeing anyone else.

Eventually, a team of three—their faces distorted behind the plastic windows in the bucket helmets of their rubber suits—approaches us carrying what look like Geiger counters.

One of them says something, but aside from the rising intonation at the end indicating that she has asked us a question, we cannot hear her.

She tries again, pressing a small walkie-talkie button sewn onto the clavicle of her hazmat gear, but it renders her voice a tiny, gnat-like buzz.

She eventually gives up and the three of them begin to run the wands over our limbs and torsos. We oblige by lifting our arms and turning around to make it easier for them.

I can be a better than adequate actor under the proper circumstances, and I've been waiting all morning to try out my role, to turn my face into a mask of distracted shock and pain.

To wince and draw shallow, labored breaths.

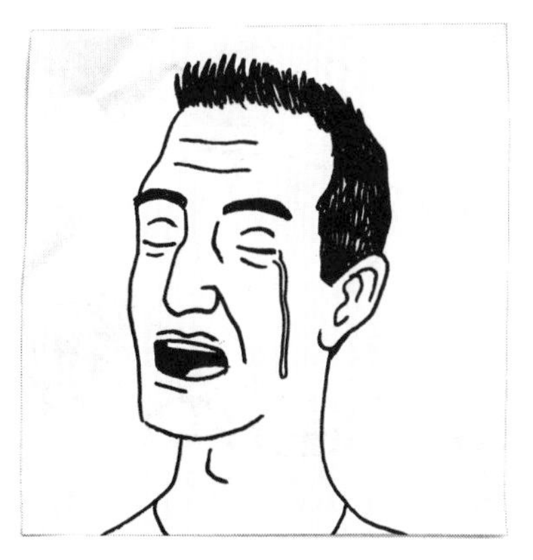

If called upon to speak, I will search for words, my Adam's apple bobbing up and down with the effort of swallowing a trickle of acrid, smoke-thickened saliva down my dry throat.

"Arms . . ." I might say. "My . . . arms. Light. Big light. Bang. Screaming."

And then I will fall silent, searching some Good Samaritan's face for an answer.

But my thespian skills don't extend to emitting radioactivity at will, so the Geiger counters remain silent.

The problem that I foresee in this imposture, one that I will have significant trouble with if anyone asks me, is portraying myself as someone who has ever been at a Mets game.

I have never been to a baseball game in my life.

Not entirely true: I went once as an eleven-year-old with my friend Mark Satok and his father.

It was my vain attempt at trying to develop an interest in heteronormative sports instead of just rooting for the star player of my favorite team:

The goddess Karen Kain, of the National Ballet of Canada.

The game was rained out before it even began and I felt giddy with reprieve.

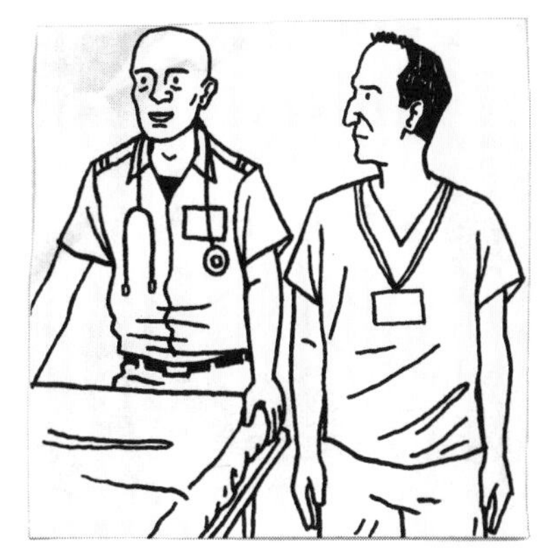

For now, though, on this deserted driveway, I've barely even had to dissemble as someone at a hospital. Eventually, we are ushered inside by an orderly and separated from one another.

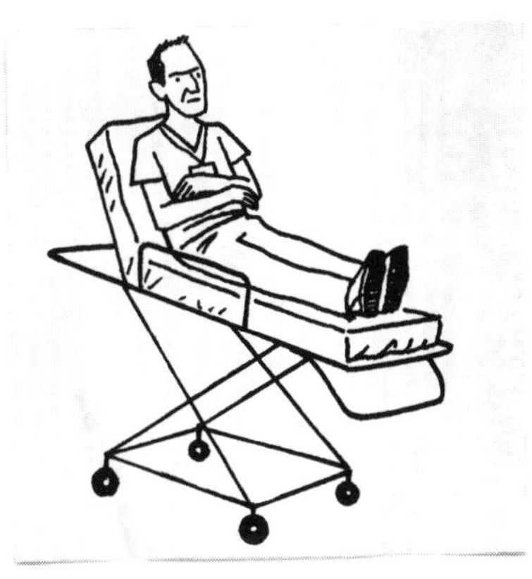

I am put on a gurney in a quiet room. It didn't occur to me to bring the newspaper.

I envisioned a breakneck exercise in barely controlled mayhem: sirens, tears, decontaminating showers at a *Silkwood* level of urgency and abrasion.

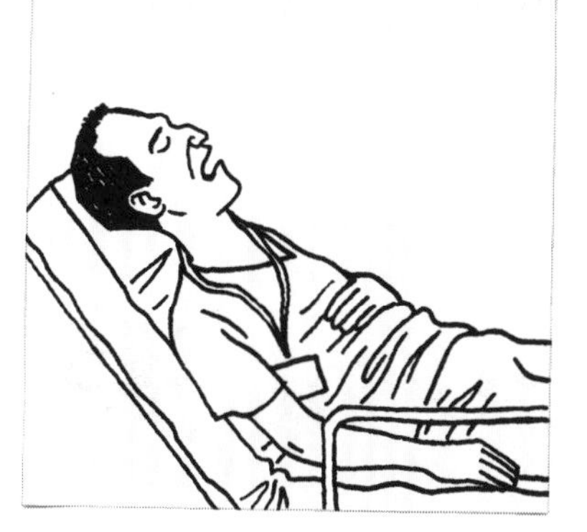

Instead, I lie there, alternately trying to count the dots in the acoustic ceiling tiles, dozing intermittently, and watching the shaft of sunlight travel across the wall.

Sometime later (forty minutes? two hours?), the same orderly comes to tell me the drill is over.

Operation United Response is a funny and counterintuitive name for anything that happens in New York City, and I have no idea if ours was successful.

I'd say it was a bit like watching someone piss himself in a pair of dark brown corduroys: an extreme gesture whose effect is largely opaque to the observer.

Given the elaborate setup and our very specific injuries, I thought we victims might have been more involved.

But again, infrastructure preparedness isn't really in my ken, so who am I to say?

I take off my paper suit, hand back my laminated card, and walk home along the quiet, decidedly nondisastrous and unexploded streets.

My forearms are restored to flesh-covered health.

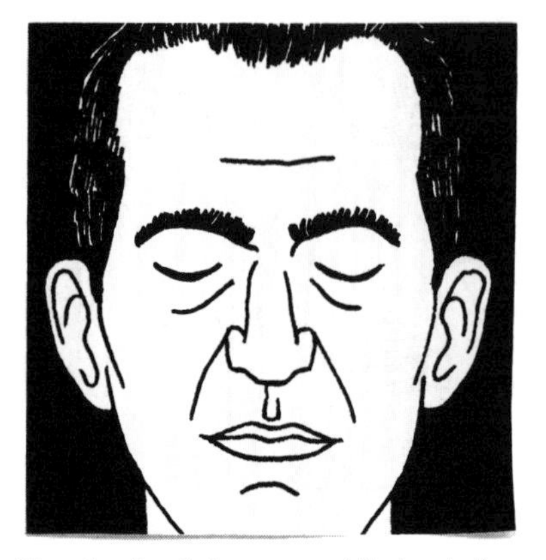

The shards of glass are spirited out of my forehead.

I could be just any other New Yorker out for a Sunday stroll wearing a bathing suit under his clothing.

LAURA
KRAFFT

The Margaret Experience
by Laura Krafft

I started following people when I was eight.

It began innocently enough. I was walking through the park when I saw an old man sitting on a bench with a rainbow of colored pens in each shirt pocket.

I don't know why but it made me want to follow him, maybe to see if he'd use the pens to write old man graffiti on walls, like "23 Skidoo!" or "I love my wife, but oh, you kid!"

Instead he just walked very slowly back to his apartment. I saw him home like a proper stalker. Even waited around to see if he'd come back out, but he never did.

No big deal, except that ever since then whenever I have some free time I like to pick random strangers and follow them. If my time is pressed I'll follow a neighbor.

As a result of this avocation, I've always felt I've had my finger on the pulse of wherever I've lived.

When I lived in New York, I knew my neighbor Louis's daughter was going to leave her husband after I followed her back to Queens and watched her wistfully read the subway ads for divorce lawyers.

In L.A., I knew that the wrinkly old Armenian man who dressed like a Sicilian extra from *The Godfather: Part II* was the one attaching stakes to my neighbor's trees late at night so the branches wouldn't grow over the sidewalk.

And in Chicago, I knew that the Belmont Avenue 7-Eleven worker with the Sikh turban liked to hang out between two Dumpsters in the alley and look at porno magazines after his shift.

So you can imagine my surprise when I learned that Margaret, the ninety-four-year-old lady who'd lived across the street from my family for my whole life had three dead siblings in her house.

Take it in for a minute. Digest it. Three dead siblings. In her house. Living with her.

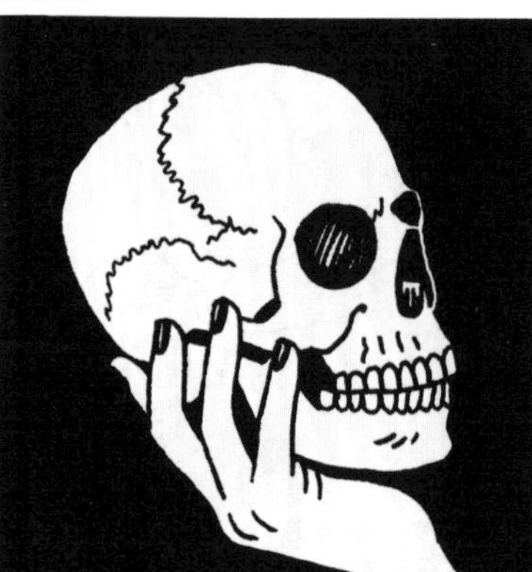

So many images conjured up. So many questions.

How did they die?

When did they die?

What were they wearing?

Were they arranged in some type of tableau? Was the tableau something beautiful like the figures in that Matisse painting *Dance*?

Or historical? Like a re-creation of the signing at Appomattox. If so, which sibling was Lee? Which one was Grant?

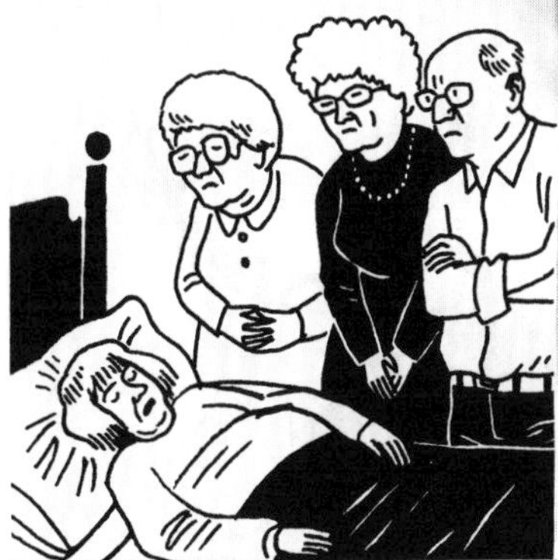

Or maybe they were just having tea. Did Margaret talk to them? Did they answer?

And what about the smell factor? Did Margaret avoid that part of the house like you avoid the refrigerator after the milk's gone bad?

It's a pretty big house. As my childhood friend and neighbor Polly said, "We should all be so lucky to have houses big enough we don't need to bury our siblings."

And perhaps most important, after the first sibling died, why didn't the other three bury him or her?

Unfortunately, the only answers that came out were sad and short.

All three siblings died of natural causes. They were found in different parts of the house. They were all covered in blankets.

After the discovery, Margaret moved into a nearby nursing home and the house was sold to a new family.

Everyone was shocked: neighbors, news reporters, deliverymen, the contractor who had recently fixed Margaret's roof. Everyone. Shocked.

But I feel confident when I say that no one was more shocked than I was.

My ego was bruised. I really thought I had a pretty good handle on the people on our block.

Mr. F.? He retired early so he could walk his dog for what seemed like twelve hours a day.

Mrs. P.? Claimed to be a socialist but secretly voted Democrat.

And Mr. S.? Obviously practiced his fly-fishing casting in the backyard to escape his unhappy marriage.

Then there was Margaret. If asked I would have said I really had her number.

I would have said she had white hair and dressed in gardening clothes. (But now that I think about it, when you're young doesn't it seem like all old people have white hair and dress in gardening clothes?)

I would have said she lived in the pretty green and white Victorian house and she loved to crouch for hours pulling weeds.

And that I knew from experience her participation in Halloween consisted of opening a pack of Saltines and giving each trick-or-treater one cracker.

As it turned out, I would have provided a pretty lousy thumbnail sketch of the lady.

The *Chicago Tribune* covered the story and featured a photo of my mother shot dramatically through a screen door so she looked like a character in a Bergman film.

She was also quoted, describing Margaret, with the old standby, "She was always very reclusive."

Quick side note: Though famous in our family's estimation, my mother has been interviewed only one other time in her life.

It was by the local news and in regard to a sex offender prowling our neighborhood.

She said, "As a mother of four daughters, I worry about rape." Which is true. She really does. Much more than she worries about murder.

"She was very reclusive," said neighbor Patricia Krafft, who has lived on Judson Avenue since 1960.

The only thing cooler than seeing my mom's name in print was having such a classic quote attributed to it. So simple. So elegant. So apt.

It sounds as if it came from someone wearing strands of pearls and reeking of lavender.

My mother wears layers of thick gold chains over a uniform of black turtlenecks.

She usually describes things in more specific and unexpected ways. For example, she'll ask after a friend of mine by saying, "How's the boy who looks like a fading matinee idol?"

Or she'll dislike an actress's performance in a film because "she looked like she was wearing dirty underwear."

For her, the smaller details of life loom large. She folds each item of her clothing into an individual Ziploc bag before putting it into a drawer.

She has been known to sit in a cab and realize she's forgotten her earrings, so she'll open her enormous purse and pull out a plastic makeup bag full of little labeled envelopes.

And she'll ask me if gold or silver goes better with her outfit. "Gold," I'll say.

And she'll flip through the envelopes until she finds one labeled "Extra Earrings—Hoops—Gold." Isn't that magnificent? It's one of my favorite things about her.

So why did she choose to describe Margaret with such a vague, Hitchcockian cool-blonde cliché like "She was always very reclusive"? It was the second most surprising part of the Margaret Experience. After the bodies.

That's what I've taken to calling it, "the Margaret Experience." And I'll admit that since it's gone down, I've been knocked off my game a bit.

Granted, I'm newly back in L.A., which is a tough city to follow people in. The houses in my new neighborhood are more hidden, so it's harder to look through people's windows.

But beyond that, I find I trust my instincts less. I don't believe what I see when I look at things from the outside as much as I used to.

The whole thing reminds me of the time I was surfing and biding my time between waves by seeing how far I could throw seaweed, when an enormous whale suddenly breached about twenty-five yards away from me.

Sure, it reminded me that we're all just flotsam on the surface of a world we can't see.

Who can get eaten by a whale at any moment.

Which, I guess, means we should always, all of us, be paddling furiously back toward the shore screaming, "What the fuck?" over and over.

And when describing people, we should always throw in the word *reclusive*.

And perhaps most important, we should just always assume everyone has a dead body or two or three in their house.

CHUCK
KLOSTERMAN
KLOSTERMAN

Burn Chuck Burn
by Chuck Klosterman

The first time I ever went to New York was sometime during the year 2000. I can't recall one thing about that particular weekend, outside of thinking that my duffel bag was too heavy.

The second time was in March 2001; this was about three months before the release of my first book.

I flew in from Ohio to meet my editor from Scribner and pretend to take meetings about the nonexistent publicity for my nonexistent book.

I was extremely enthusiastic and confused by everything. I thought I was a genius because I already knew who the Strokes were, even though their first album wasn't due until September 25.

I assumed such insight would electrify people. This proved false.

I quickly realized that not only were people unimpressed by this knowledge, but the Strokes were already so famous that everyone appeared to have haircuts exactly like theirs.

The Lower Manhattan streets were saturated with hundreds of kids who looked like lesser Strokes.

It was like a boatload of refugees had founded a hermetic community called Casablancaville, where the only available foods were pizza, sandwiches, and secondhand neckties.

I was not a citizen of this place. I had non-Strokes hair, no beard, and very round eyeglasses. I think I might have been wearing cargo pants.

I do know the first two bars I visited were named Siberia and KGB.

This gave me the erroneous impression that all Manhattan taverns are modeled after the Soviet Union.

The third bar I patronized was a train-themed dive called the Boxcar Lounge, where I was scheduled to meet my editor and several of his friends.

It took me a long time to get there because I kept giving the cab driver the bar's exact street address and he kept asking, "But what are the cross streets?" I assumed his question was rhetorical.

When I finally arrived at the bar, I located my editor (who looks a lot like John-Boy from *The Waltons*) and began chatting with all his friends and colleagues.

Everyone was drinking heavily and acting over-the-top affable. My confidence was soaring, because I felt like I was finally making it in life.

I felt indestructible and insane and devoid of worry. I was acting like a person on cocaine, except I was not on cocaine. I kept delivering intense, boorish, nonsensical proclamations.

"If you buy your child a bed that looks like a race car," I argued.

"Don't complain when he becomes an adult and dies in an auto accident."

I went on a detailed diatribe about how the average height of the American male is actually much higher than the typically reported five feet nine.

This figure is based on the premise that dwarfs and midgets are represented more frequently than nonfamous giants.

I accused a total stranger of arson, then manslaughter. It was a wonderful night, at least for me.

I kept initiating banter with a woman who sometimes described herself as an actress and sometimes described herself as a museum employee.

For whatever reason, I was convinced she resembled a Runaways-era Lita Ford.

Around eleven thirty, I was sitting at a table and staring at Young Lita Ford while she bought a few drinks at the bar.

Suddenly, the (previously rude and noncommunicative) bartender she was speaking with jumped on top of the bar like a surfer.

He loudly sang a few lines from that song by Joe Jackson that goes, "Is she really going out with him? Is she really going to take him home tonight?"

He seemed to be looking directly at me.

I probably assumed it was some kind of colorful, outside-the-rhombus East Coast marketing ploy. Maybe this was how all Manhattan bartenders behaved.

Months later, I was informed that Young Lita Ford had told this bartender I was her boyfriend.

Assumably because I was the weirdest, most grotesque person in the bar.

Which, in theory, would confuse the barkeep and stop him from hitting on her every time she purchased a drink.

I suspect there were lots of things going on in this establishment that I was not aware of.

Now, it was around this time that I started making (and repeating) a colossal mistake. Due to my unquenchable confidence, I was buying a lot of drinks.

I was giving drinks to the same strangers I was accusing of manslaughter.

And all my life, I'd thought I understood the process of tipping bartenders—I thought you always tipped at the end.

That's how it was in every other place I'd ever lived: You would buy drinks all night, and then tip the bartender (or the waitress) with a ten- or twenty-dollar bill at the evening's conclusion.

The idea of tipping a dollar for every single drink you buy in real time had never occurred to me. It's a totally reasonable policy, but at the time it was completely foreign to me.

So what I was doing was this: I was constantly going up to a troll-like bartender who already hated me, ordering four beers at five dollars apiece, and dismissively giving the bartender a twenty-dollar bill.

Then I would stoically walk away. I probably did this four or five times in a row. I fully intended to tip him at the *end* of the night, but (of course) he didn't know this.

He just had to stand there, un-tipped, while I seduced Young Lita Ford with lava-hot gems of sexualized wisdom like:

"You know who's fucking underrated? James fucking Madison."

At some point in the evening (2:00 a.m.? 4:00 a.m.?), I staggered up to the bartender to buy four final drinks and (at long last) tip the angry dude who'd been feeding me beer all night.

But before I could order, the bartender asked me a question. "Who are you, by the way?"

I was surprised he cared. "I'm Chuck," I said. "You can call me Chuck. That's what everyone calls me. My name is Chuck!"

"OK, Chuck," he said. "I hope you fucking die tonight."

"What?"

"I hope you die in the street, Chuck. I hope you never make it back to wherever the hell you're from, Chuck. I hope they find your body in a basement, Chuck."

This short, round, vaguely rockabilly bartender proceeded to unleash an avalanche of single-minded vitriol upon my inebriated skull, not unlike the opening sequence of *Full Metal Jacket*.

His use of directive address struck me as extra menacing. I kept trying to apologize, but every time I tried, he just talked louder.

Finally—and this, I think, is what made the man brilliant—he put his fists in the air and spontaneously started *chanting*: "Burn Chuck burn! Burn Chuck burn!"

I could instantly tell the sentiment was going to catch on. It had a natural rhythm.

There were a bunch of wholly uninvolved, assumably obliterated strangers sitting at the Boxcar bar, and they got swept up in the anti-Chuck fever: "Burn Chuck burn! Burn Chuck burn!"

It was like an abortion rally. In a matter of seconds, everyone in the bar was chanting, "Burn Chuck burn!"

Including people who were (just that very moment) walking into the establishment without any idea of a) what was going on or b) who Chuck was.

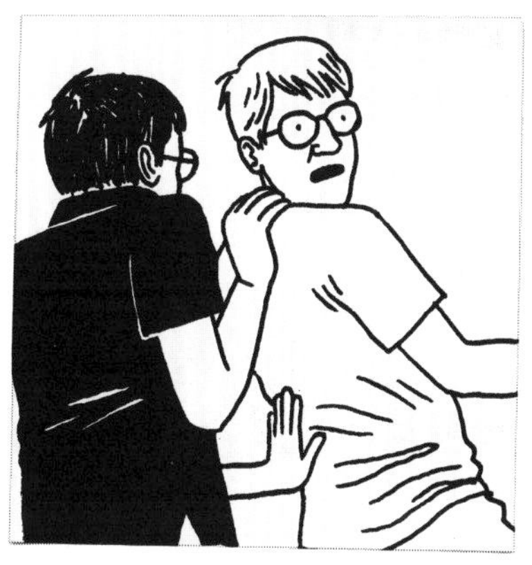

My twenty-seven-year-old editor, fearing the possible murder of an unpublished author, which would have been difficult to explain to his boss, hustled me out the door.

As we walked north on Avenue B with Young Lita Ford and the remaining members of our party, we could faintly hear the drunkards still inside Boxcar.

They refused to relent from their arbitrary, bloodthirsty battle cry:

"Burn Chuck burn! Burn Chuck burn! Burn Chuck burn!"

It was at that point I decided I should move to New York.

DANIEL
ENGBER

Cow the Bird
by Daniel Engber

If my mother was killing off my pets one by one with her bare hands, then at least she made it look natural.

An intestinal parasite, a kidney stone, too many fish flakes; the animals had a habit of dying when I wasn't around.

There was the fish—a minnow scooped from the Hudson River—who vanished one afternoon from the coffee jar on the windowsill.

And the guinea pig, Ralphette, who disappeared from her cage in the middle of the night.

By the time I woke up, she was wrapped in paper towels and newspaper, sealed in a Ziploc bag, and wedged in the back of the freezer.

Mom was the animal undertaker, pressing tiny eyelids closed with her fingertips while the rest of us were sleeping.

I was over at a friend's house on the night she came for the bird.

Cow—that's my parakeet—spent two years in a cage next to my desk, with a mirror affixed to the bars.

He would be the first of many birds to pass a short, miserable life under my care, but at the time he seemed like a special case.

A sad sack. I remember him chirping at his own reflection, and spitting up mouthfuls of seed so the mirror bird would have something to eat.

As long as we lived together, Cow never once sang a note. He honked, though, at high volume, interrupting my homework and keeping me up at night.

If he'd been able to mimic human speech—like parakeets are supposed to—he might have learned the phrase *shut the hell up*, or the words *die, die, die.*

When the bird was healthy, I tried to browbeat him into getting sick.

When he got sick, I did what I could to make him better.

We brought Cow to the vet when a clump of dried guano began to accumulate on his backside.

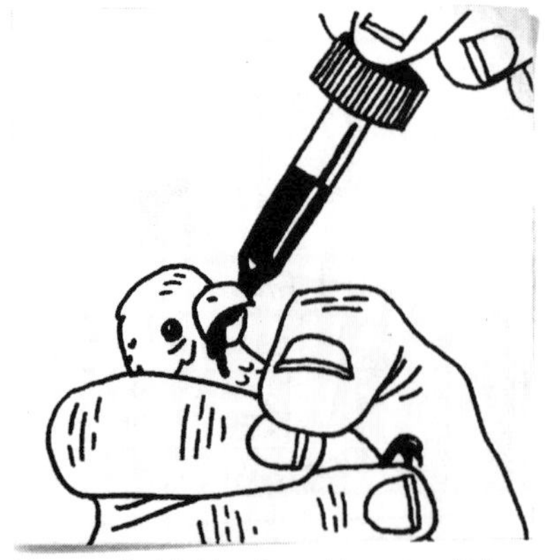

He wasn't drinking from his water dish, so we had to feed him medicine through an eyedropper, forcing the fluid into his beak until it bubbled from his nostrils.

I left my mother in charge of this treatment on the night I went to David's house.

When I got home the next day, Cow was twelve hours frozen. He'd drowned on the antibiotics, my mother told me.

I believed that story of a death by good intentions for half my life. It seemed like a parable of what happens when guilt starts to feel like love.

But it wasn't true. Cow hadn't died because we'd tried too hard to save him. He had been murdered.

My mother had taken his hollow-boned head between her thumb and forefinger and twisted until his neck broke.

A word on methodology: There are plenty of humane ways to kill a full-grown parakeet.

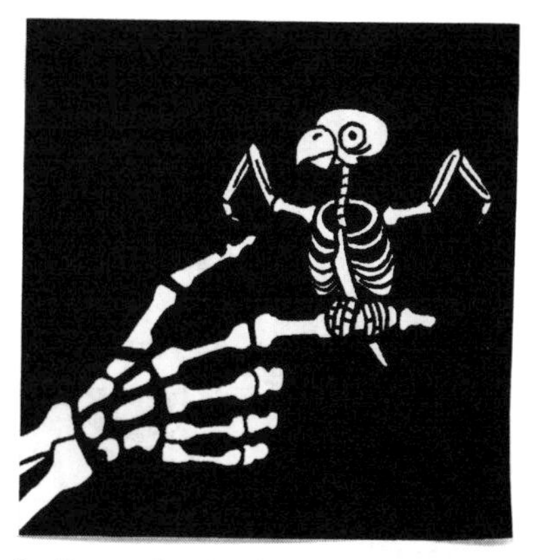

Poultry professionals use metal tongs to wring birds' necks, or they drop the animals in electrified water pools, or carbon dioxide tents, or wood chippers.

When the British government culled six million farm animals during a foot-and-mouth outbreak in 2001, the military officer in charge said it took more planning than the Gulf War.

One member of Parliament suggested gathering the animals together and then dropping napalm on the heath.

My mother has always been good with her hands, though. She's artsy-craftsy. In the old days, she played guitar and wore her hair like Joan Baez.

Now she spends her time making quilts for her grandchildren.

In between, when I was growing up, she was a chain-smoking Wall Street executive.

Her colleagues wore tweed and bowties; she wore a silver necklace from Santa Fe decked out with grizzly bear claws.

It was fifteen years before I learned the real story of Cow's demise. My dad—the only living witness to the crime—gave his testimony at Thanksgiving dinner.

My mother had entered my room with the eyedropper, he explained between bites of roast turkey.

She'd planned to administer the dose of ornacycline according to protocol. But she found the pitiful bird lying on the bottom of its cage, puffing its feathers.

She put down the eyedropper and snapped its neck.

My mom corroborated the story, and then assured us she'd made no other attempts on the lives of family pets.

Whether she was guilty of serial euthanasia or she'd merely whisked away the animal corpses before anyone saw them, we all knew that she had done her best to make death invisible.

Cow the bird was living in my bedroom until the night when he wasn't. That's how we dealt with tragedy: When people got sick, they disappeared.

I remember one day my brother was gone from the apartment.

Then all of a sudden he was back, with a bandage over one eye. I found out later—months later—that he'd had a brain tumor.

The Thanksgiving confession came as a shock, though I'd just spent months killing animals myself.

As a graduate student in neurobiology, I'd cut open the brains of mice, kittens, and monkeys; dozens of living things had died in my hands.

But in the end, it was the birds that drove me away from science. They lived in the basement, in cages stacked three high.

Our lab was studying the Bengalese finch, a songbird that's known for musical improvisation.

Other species, such as the zebra finch, learn one tune in childhood and repeat it forever after; the Bengalese likes to riff.

Most of the studies involved putting a male and a female in the same cage and listening to the courtship songs.

Sometimes we recorded from their brains using electrodes.

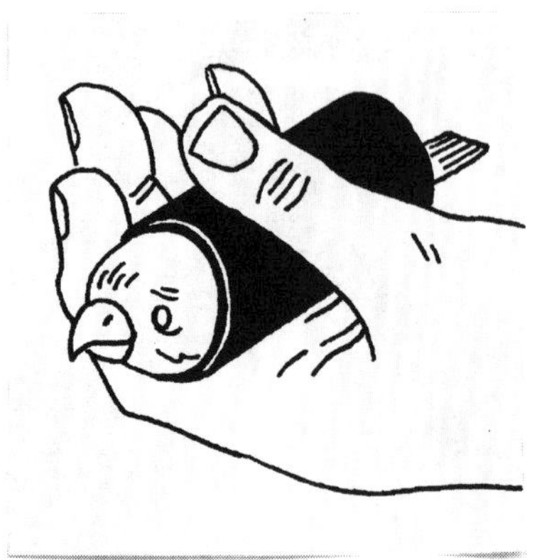

But my job, the one assigned to me when I joined the lab, was to conduct a more invasive experiment:

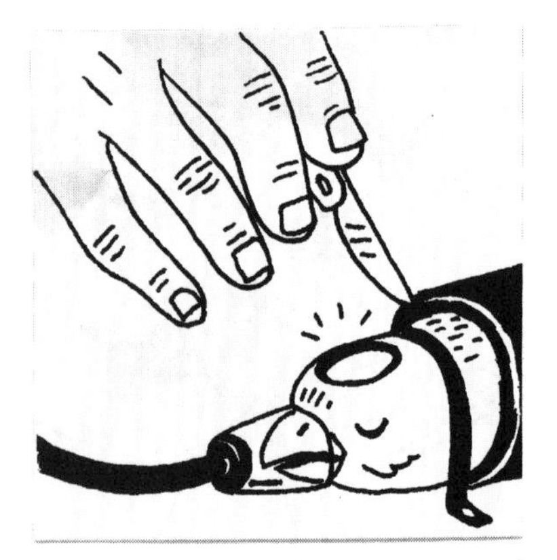

A gross excavation of the avian neuroanatomy, and wholesale removal of its cerebellum.

If I succeeded and the bird survived, how well would it sing?

I spent weeks practicing on live subjects, as one after another succumbed to fatal hemorrhages.

After a while, it started to feel like a career unto itself: Every day, I'd wake up at 8:00 a.m., eat breakfast, pack a sandwich, and head into the lab to kill more birds.

We'd clamp a finch to the table, place a halothane gas mask over its beak, and start plucking the feathers from its head.

One bird would be dead by lunchtime, and then another would die in the afternoon.

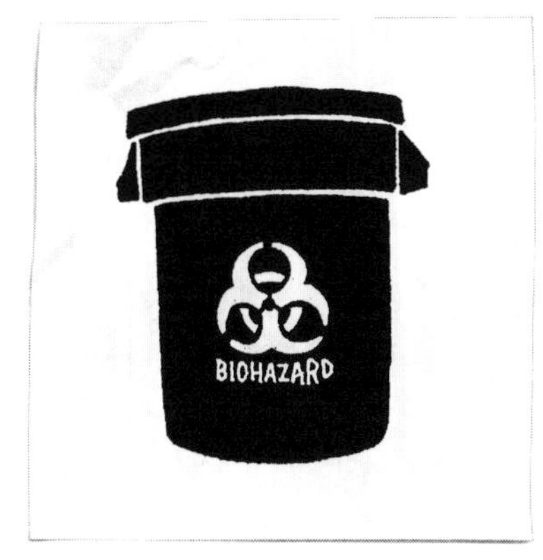

A small flock of cadavers piled up in the biohazard bin, until eventually my technique improved.

A few birds even survived the operation. Back in their cages, they'd wobble to their feet with bits of seed stuck to their scalps.

And then I'd watch, taking notes, as they tottered in circles, around and around, until they died. Not one of them ever sang a note.

If my mother was Jack Kevorkian, then I was Josef Mengele.

Now, I suppose my own history of violence should have helped put Cow's story in perspective.

That was a mercy killing, a coup de grâce, while the finches in my lab had been in perfect health.

But somehow the brain studies only made my mom's betrayal seem worse. She'd killed my parakeet so I wouldn't have to see an animal die.

And then I found myself in the middle of a Bengalese massacre.

I don't know if I'd have been any wiser for seeing Cow wither away in his cage.

It's not like my mother had deprived me of some developmental milestone—a first dead animal, or a bar mitzvah pet murder.

Still, I couldn't shake the feeling that the woman who was playing the role of my mom had gone wildly off script.

Here's how a mother stays in character: She takes you to the beach and drapes you with seaweed.

She makes you cinnamon toast.

She dresses you as Pinocchio for Halloween.

On your eighth birthday, she comes into your room with a blindfold, and when you take it off twenty minutes later you're at the pet store.

And here's how a mom scares the shit out of you: She buys that little green bird with the speckled crown, and breaks its neck.

Knowing Cow's fate wouldn't have kept me from going to graduate school, or from suctioning out finch brains with a vacuum tube. But I do wish Cow's death hadn't been such a secret.

I wish I'd seen my mom in action, like one of those women who finds her baby under the wheels of a 4x4 and suddenly gains Hulk-like strength.

Maybe my mom sensed that I was in a certain kind of danger back then, and she transformed, for an evening, into someone else. Instead of turning super strong she turned super tough.

It's a horrible thing to crush a small animal to death. Believe me, I know.

In the end, I guess that's what makes it so special. There's nothing like a mother's love.

KRISTEN
SCHAAL

Miss Peppermint Twist
by Kristen Schaal

I've been attracted to the bright lights of New York City ever since I saw *The Muppets Take Manhattan* when I was six.

I knew that I had to do whatever it took to make it in the Big Apple, even if it meant living in a bus locker and befriending rats.

I just wanted to be on Broadway with my future best friends.

Fifteen years later, I made my move.

The secret to New York is you have to put your time in. It's more costly than any other city, and the currency is tenacity.

I was trying to get auditions and attempting to collect best friends to do shows with. It was slow going.

I didn't have a lot of money, and was on a strict diet of one slice of pizza for lunch.

And one 16-ounce can of malt liquor for dinner. It filled me up and took the edge off being poor.

I have one can of Crazy Horse malt liquor that I saved from that time.

They don't make it anymore because it's racist.

In my daydreams I crack that dusty can open as an old woman sunning my sagging tits on the French Riviera.

I will have to toast Crazy Horse.

I attempted many jobs to afford real food. But the worst job by far was as a character at FAO Schwarz.

FAO casts actors to walk around the store as characters to create an "experience"—an experience that helps them sell toys for almost twice the price of Toys"R"Us.

Also, seeing Barbie walk around with Alice in Wonderland is incredibly magical. Almost taboo—what are they doing together?

Fairy tales shouldn't mix. They're sold separately.

The character I auditioned for was an original one they had created specifically for the FAO Schweetz shop, called Ms. Peppermint Twist.

Ms. Peppermint Twist was there to assist the customers with whatever candy needs they had and elevate the candy-buying experience to an even sweeter level. If that's possible!

It's no surprise that I nailed the part. I am Frederick August Otto Schwarz's wet dream, if he's dreaming of character actors.

I look like a fusion of Sandra Bernhard and Shirley Temple.

My voice is spectacularly odd.

It was only a matter of time before this unique vessel I navigate crashed into a gimmicky toy store.

I had to wear a pink wig, pink sunglasses, striped stockings, and a tutu. I had to wear it all for six hours at a time. I had to act like I was into it.

It was a nightmare. I would never advocate drinking on the job. Unless your job description is pretending to be happy in a tutu as you guide a fat child to choose between Swedish Fish and Nerd Rope.

If that is your job, then I would recommend shot-gunning *two* Icehouse beers prior to clocking in. That's right, I said *two* beers. I could afford it because I was employed.

I did have some artistic freedom. It was my job to come up with my character's background.

I decided that Ms. Peppermint Twist was an orphan. Her mom had left her in FAO, very much like Punky Brewster, except this sad girl hadn't found her Henry Warnimont.

Instead, she'd stumbled into a giant cotton candy vat in the basement, which burned her severely and gave her pink hair.

Mentally out of sorts from the trauma of the cotton candy accident, she had allowed the owners of FAO to enslave her to work in the candy shop for the rest of her days.

When customers asked for her story, that's what she told them, following up with: "That's why I'm so tired, because I had to stay up all night making the candy for you and now I have to stand here and watch you buy it."

I never got the actual numbers, but it is my belief that guilty candy purchases increased significantly under Ms. Twist's reign.

Now, I don't want to come off as one of those people who complains about working. I will suck it up and work.

And my patchwork résumé will prove that I will take any job. But in order to survive most jobs, you need to have the opportunity to zone out.

Your body continues to work but your mind escapes to a place where you can acknowledge your dissatisfaction. Those soul-saving moments to mumble your discontent under your breath as you toil are necessary.

Imagine if you saw Ms. Peppermint Twist having that quiet moment in the Schweetz shop. It would be unsettling. And so she wasn't allowed any.

But one day it happened. It was slow in the Schweetz shop. I had just eaten a handful of chewy peach things and my guard was down as I leaned against the counter.

I was reflecting on how I hoped the terrorists wouldn't destroy America's oldest toy store, melting me down in a sticky pink wig.

I was thinking about my coworkers: Barbie, who took private en pointe ballet lessons to prepare for the release of Nutcracker Barbie.

And the Toy Soldier who'd impregnated Alice in Wonderland (they weren't in Wonderland when it happened; I believe they were in Queens).

I was absentmindedly running my tongue over the two cavities I had acquired from the free candy perk when one of the FAO managers—a round, moist man—happened to walk by and notice that my mind was far away from candy.

"Ms. Peppermint Twist, this is not how you sell the candy!"

"Oh."

"It's like this!" And he began boisterously welcoming everyone within earshot to the Schweetz shop, announcing its goodness and handing out empty candy bags with such overwhelming joy my cavities started to throb.

"Now, you do it!" He turned to me after his minute-long demonstration, panting slightly from the exertion.

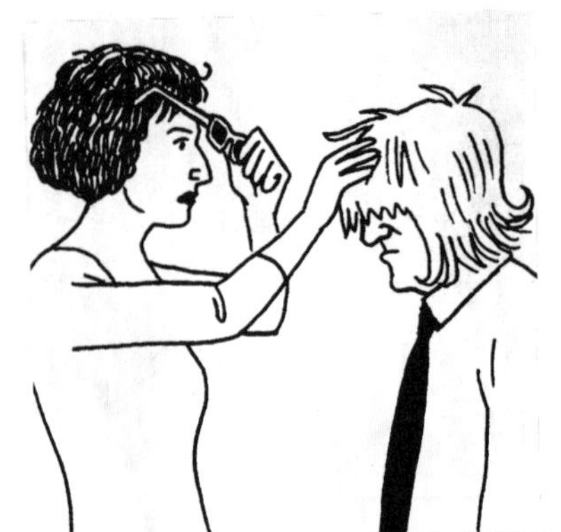

"I don't know, sir. It's like watching Meryl Streep. I'm never going to be that good. It's pointless to even try. I think you should be wearing a wig and sunglasses, sir."

He didn't agree with my praise.

And shortly after I was laid off from the worst job of my life.

As for Ms. Peppermint Twist, I can only guess that she is still in that basement, giving a hundred percent to the Man.

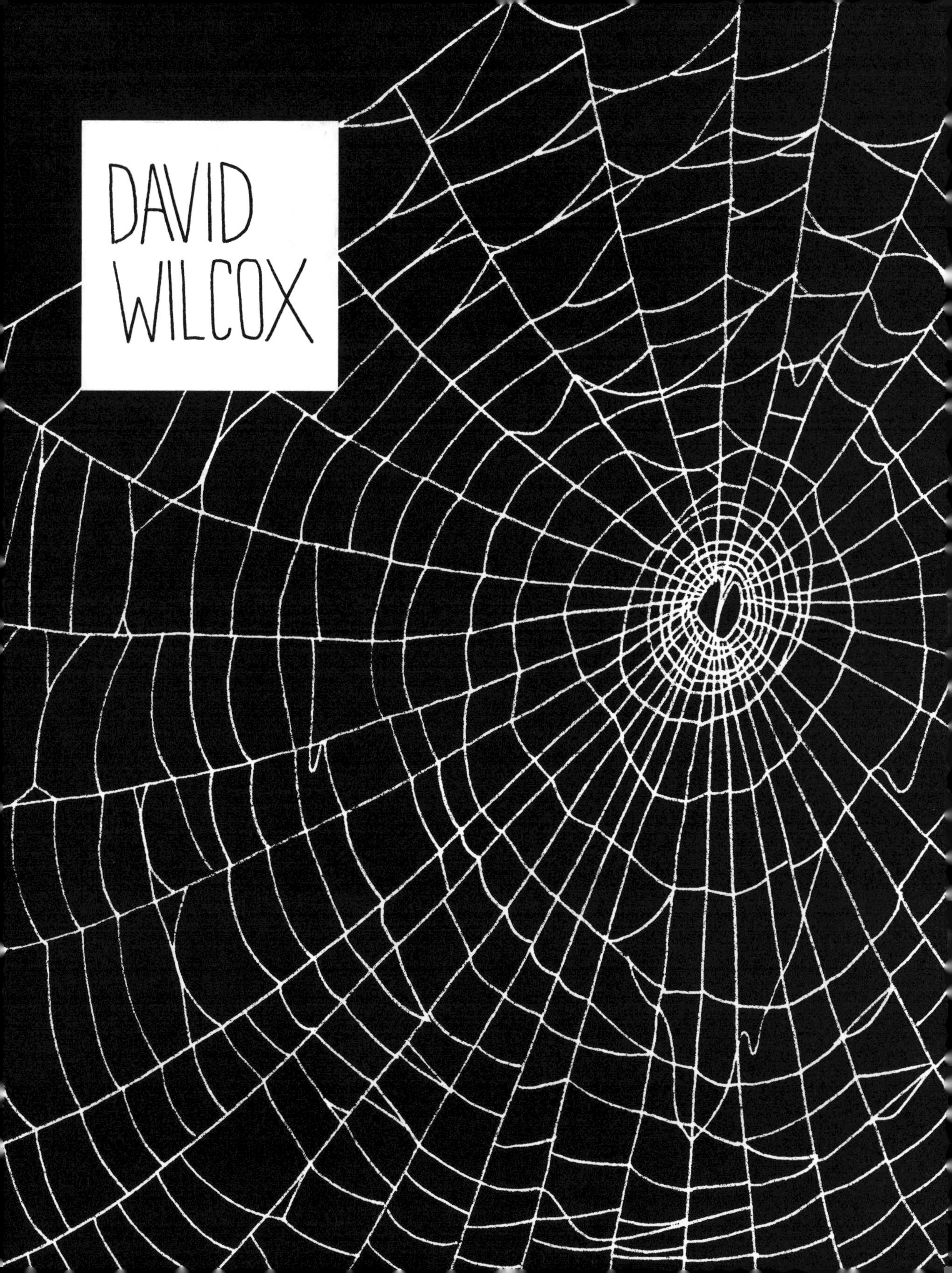

DAVID
WILCOX

Cancer Spider
by David Wilcox

The first thing you should know about my landlord, Jeff, is he's a compassionate man.

The second thing you should know is he's homosexual. I say this because with Jeff compassion and homosexuality go hand in hand.

Meaning: If you're a man, and you're in need, and you're willing to have sex with another man—specifically Jeff—he will help you out.

I met Jeff shortly after I moved to Chicago, when I started renting the apartment directly beneath his.

I liked Jeff, but I couldn't help but notice that the company he kept skewed to the unsavory.

He was getting on in years, his health wasn't great, and his last long-term relationship hadn't ended well, so Jeff had more or less given up on love.

Instead, he made time with one down-on-his-luck stud after another, offering them free room and board for . . . well, the things I could usually hear them doing upstairs.

Some of Jeff's companions stuck around for months; others, merely days. I rarely knew their names or circumstances.

One was a South American art student who planted a bunch of penis sculptures in the garden.

Another was an Ed Begley Jr. look-alike who stained the building's decks while dressed in nothing but boxer-briefs.

The rest were an interchangeable cast of tan, muscular drifters. Cabana boys in search of a cabana.

The only guy who didn't fit the mold was a pot-bellied ex-con Jeff flew up from Georgia one summer to paint our building.

The story I heard from one of my neighbors, who knew Jeff better than I, was that Jeff had met the ex-con through a prison pen-pals program.

The ex-con wasn't gay, or at least didn't identify as such, but while he was locked up he occasionally sent Jeff dirty letters as a thank-you for the money Jeff had deposited in his commissary account.

I didn't know if Jeff and the ex-con were actually fooling around or not. I didn't really want to think about it.

In truth, I didn't want to think about the ex-con at all. Maybe it was his decaying teeth and the janky Grim Reaper tattoo on his neck.

Maybe it was the little things I overheard him say on his cell phone, things like, "I can't do that cocaine no more."

"If I do that cocaine, they'll take my babies away, and you ain't gonna take my babies away."

Or maybe it's just that, as a thirty-year resident of Texas whose entire extended family hails from Alabama, I've spent enough time around rednecks to know I don't care to spend any more.

One night, not long after the ex-con showed up, I noticed something unusual in our yard. It was one of those signs contractors display while they're on a job.

PAINTING&OTHER

428-555-8218

Except this one was fashioned from a discarded cabinet door and a stick of plywood. It read PAINTING & OTHER across the top, and there was a phone number—the ex-con's, presumably.

I guess he was feeling entrepreneurial.

There was also, for reasons I never understood, a drawing of a bucktoothed arachnid with the words CANCER SPIDER scrawled beneath it.

That's what I called the ex-con from that moment forward: Cancer Spider.

Cancer Spider and I only had one conversation of any length. It took place on a Sunday afternoon. I was sitting on my deck, reading a book and drinking a beer.

Cancer Spider was painting the interior of the vacant apartment next to mine. He stepped outside at one point for a cigarette break, saw me, and sauntered over.

The first thing he said was, "I'd sure like to buy one of those beers." I told him I'd be happy to just give him one. "Nah," he said. "Told the man I wouldn't drink while I'm staying with him."

I muttered a reply—"Oh well," or something like that—and turned my attention back to my book. But Cancer Spider was feeling chatty.

"So what you got for nightlife around here?" "Just bars, mostly," I said. "Sorta depends on what you're looking for."

Cancer Spider cleared his throat. "Well," he said, lowering his voice, "I need a ho."

And in case there was any confusion as to why he might need this ho, he added, "I feel the need to spread my seed."

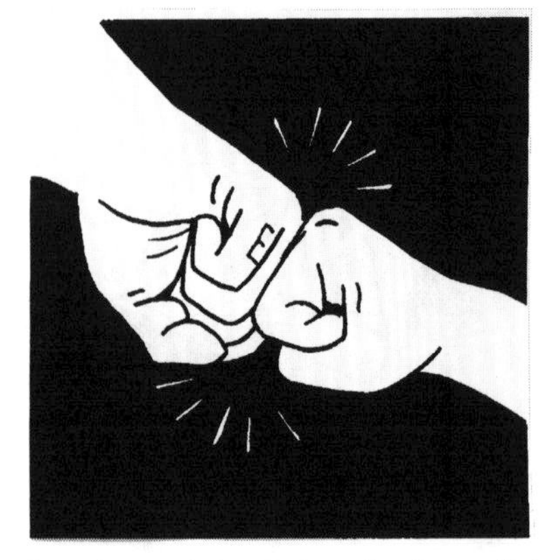

I'm not sure what sort of reaction Cancer Spider was expecting. A fist bump?

Maybe he was hoping I kept a little black book like the one Sam had on *Cheers* and that I could hook him up with his choice of bimbos.

But I didn't say or do anything. I just kept reading. "What you into?" he asked.

"What do you mean?"
"You like girls?"
"Yeah."

"All right! I'll find you this weekend and we gonna tear it up!"

"Actually, this weekend's no good," I said. "My friend's having breast-reduction surgery and I offered to help her out. I know that sounds like a lie, but it's not."

For the record, it was a lie. And feeling the tiniest bit guilty for telling it, I offered to suggest some places where Cancer Spider might get lucky.

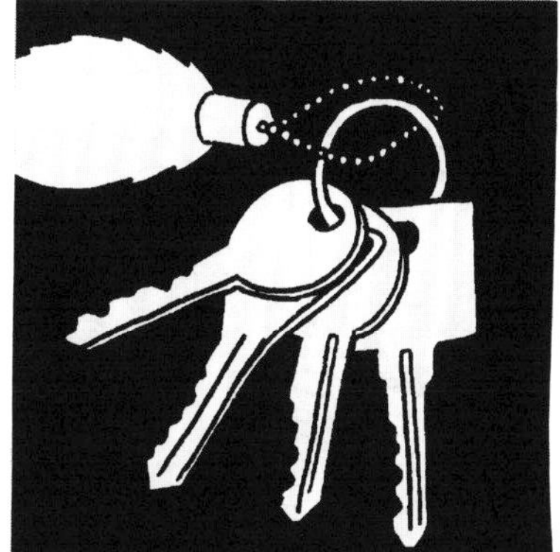

"That won't work," he said. "If I get shitfaced, I can't go back to Jeff's." He considered his options, then said, "How 'bout you loan me a key to your house?"

"I don't think it's a good idea for me to get involved," I said. "If Jeff doesn't want you drinking, I don't want him to think I'm enabling you."

Cancer Spider furrowed his brow. He was either considering my logic or he was trying to figure out what "enabling" meant. Finally he shrugged his shoulders and said, "That makes sense."

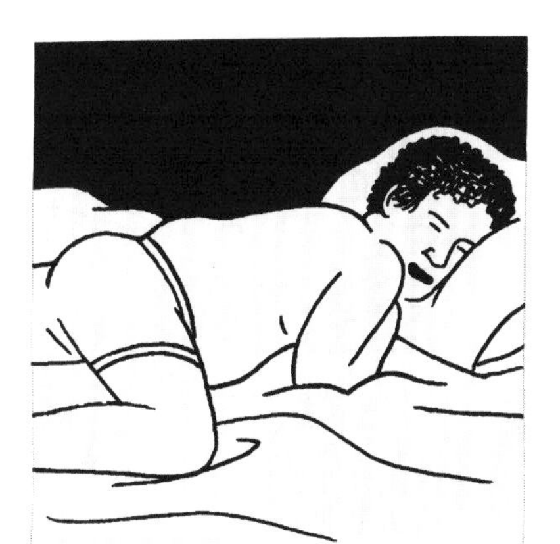

The next morning I woke up dripping with sweat. It was late August and brutally hot, so I'd slept in boxers with no shirt.

Years prior I might have slept naked, but as I've gotten older I've developed an aversion to nude sleep, even if the sleep follows sex.

Actually, scratch that—*especially* if the sleep follows sex. Reason being: In the heat of the moment, no one gives much thought to what you really look like without your clothes on. There's too much happening.

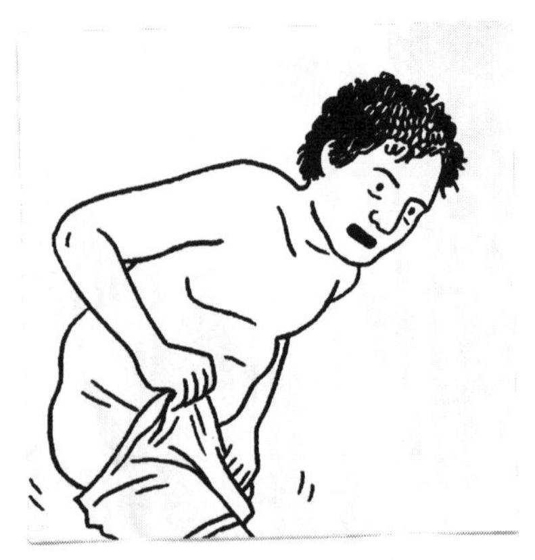

The next morning, however, there's *nothing* happening. There's all the time in the world to just *look*. And nudity does not flatter me.

Anyway. I got up, half-naked and half-asleep, and stumbled to the bathroom, passing a gigantic window along the way.

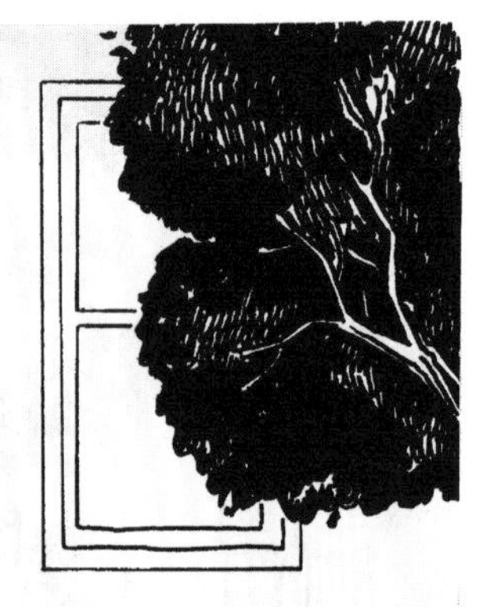

I never bothered covering that window with curtains or blinds, because I lived on the second floor, and when the trees were in bloom, the leaves and limbs provided near-total privacy.

To see inside that window, someone would have to be pressed up against the glass, some thirty feet in the air. It just so happens, however, that on this particular morning that's exactly where Cancer Spider was.

Standing atop a ladder, holding a can of paint, with an unobstructed head-to-toe view of me in my underwear.

He stopped working and stared. I froze. And then, accepting that the worst was over, I waved. He waved back. And we both went about our business.

While I splashed water on my face and wiped the crud out of my eyes in the bathroom, I heard Cancer Spider shout to no one in particular:

"Just saw the man in his underwear. *Horrible* sight."

I realized it wasn't personal. I could've looked like Marky Mark from the Funky Bunch and Cancer Spider's reaction would have been the same.

And yet still I found myself wondering, "Why didn't he like looking at me? Do I really look *horrible*? What, I'm not his type? *That* fat piece of shit? Who the hell does he think he is?!"

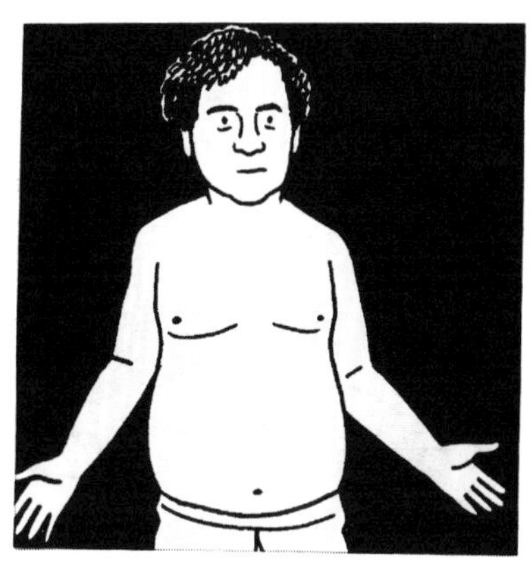

But the real reason it stung so bad was that Cancer Spider confirmed something I knew deep down but refused to admit: I was letting myself go.

And the reason for that had everything to do with the apartment I was standing in.

I was originally supposed to move to Chicago with my girlfriend. We'd spent ten years together, all of them in Texas, and we were both ready for a change.

Chicago was my idea. Initially she was hesitant, seeing as neither of us had a job there, so we decided I would move first and once I was settled, she would follow.

Only she never did. Not long after I signed the lease on Jeff's vacant apartment, she broke up with me, at which point our new place became my new place.

A place that was haunted from the start by the ghost of a life that had never existed.

The five years I'd spent in that apartment were the loneliest I'd ever endured. Loneliness had led to apathy, apathy had led to drinking, and drinking had led to flab.

Not that anyone ever made me feel bad about it, because I was living in Chicago—and if there are three things a Chicagoan will never judge, they're apathy, drinking, and flab.

I saw Cancer Spider a few more times in the weeks that followed, but we never spoke again. He finished painting our building and eventually Jeff put him on a flight back to Georgia.

Not long after, I told Jeff I was moving out. He said he was sorry to lose me as a tenant, but that he'd also just refinanced his mortgage, saving a bundle.

"So I'm not sure what I'll do with your place," he told me. "I might just keep it as a guest apartment. It'd be nice to have a place where people could stay for longer periods of time."

I told him to let me know what he decided, because I had friends who might be interested in taking over my lease. But he didn't seem to hear me. "It's important," he continued, "the older you get."

"What is?" I asked.

"Company."

NEIL
deGRASSE
TYSON

Romancing the Mountaintop
by Neil deGrasse Tyson

"I know that I am mortal by nature, and ephemeral; but when I trace, at my pleasure, the windings to and fro of the heavenly bodies I no longer touch earth with my feet: I stand in the presence of Zeus himself and take my fill of ambrosia." —Claudius Ptolemy

I have never met Zeus, nor have I ever tasted ambrosia, but I am no less seduced by the offerings of the universe than Ptolemy was in the second century AD.

Once or twice each year I travel to a mountaintop telescope like the one at the Cerro Tololo Inter-American Observatory (CTIO) in the Andes Mountains of Chile.

The nighttime sky of the southern hemisphere offers a different view of the cosmos than from the north.

CTIO is at a 30° southern latitude, and in June the galactic center of the Milky Way passes directly above it at midnight.

A large part of my research is about a region near the Milky Way's center known as the "galactic bulge," made up of more than ten billion stars—about ten percent of the galaxy's total.

When observing galaxies, one can typically identify only the brightest of its giant stars. The remaining billions blur into puddles of light.

The powerful CTIO telescope allows for observation of these remaining stars, providing a unique platform to understand the structure and formation of all spiral galaxies like our own.

My pilgrimage from Princeton, New Jersey, to the summit of Cerro Tololo takes three days and is a combination of long plane flights, boring layovers, and hazardous taxi rides and bus trips.

My trek has no less drama but is certainly much shorter than the journeys of the photons I'm observing, whose journeys began in the galactic bulge about twenty-six thousand years ago.

Our two paths through space and time converge at the focal plane of the telescope.

The photons that narrowly miss the telescope's giant mirror end their journey by slamming into the mountainside.

But those I snatch from the photon stream are the basis for nearly all my research.

We analyze data collected at the telescope by computer, using methods similar to those of paleontologists who interpret time using fossil evidence.

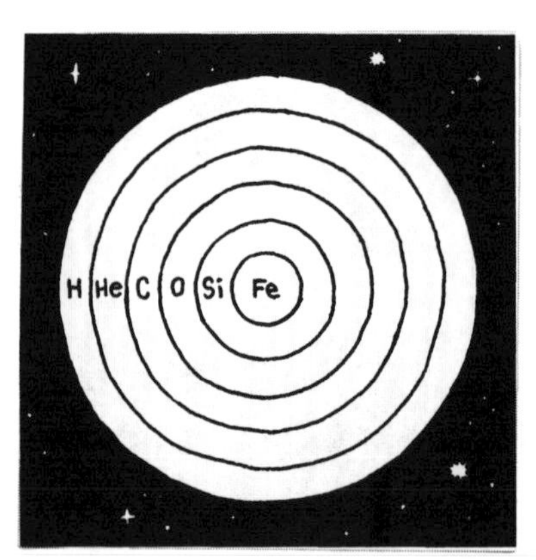

We infer the history of the galactic bulge from the heavy-element enrichments dispersed among its stars.

The Big Bang created gas clouds that formed the first generation of stars composed of pure hydrogen and helium.

Elements heavier than hydrogen and helium were created later, within high-mass stars that end their lives in explosions we call supernovae.

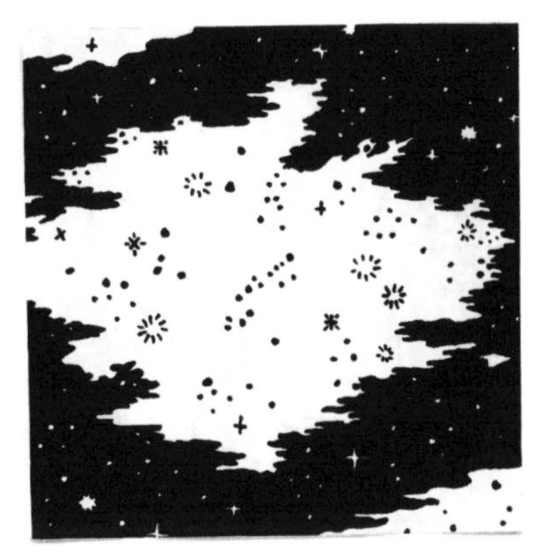

These heavy elements mixed with gas clouds that formed the next generation of stars.

This cycle continues, as each generation of stars becomes more and more enriched with heavy elements.

Some stars die shortly after they are born, but most live for many billions of years. The galactic bulge is a beehive mixture of different stellar generations.

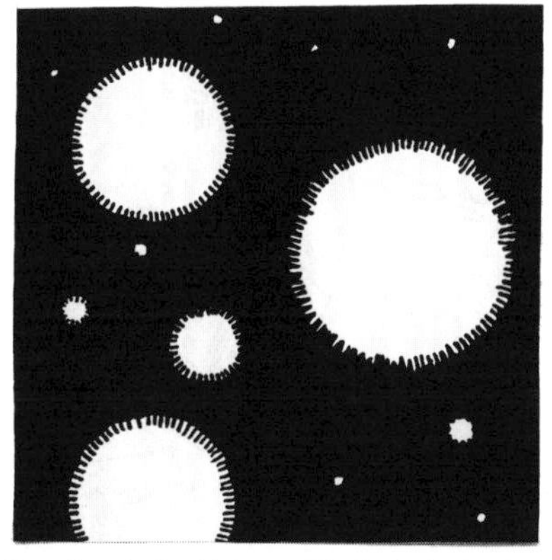

To untangle the history of the bulge's star formation we compare the number of older stars with a low abundance of heavy elements to the number of newer stars with high heavy-element abundance.

We tag each star with a velocity in space and a location in the galaxy, deriving information about the mass, gravity, and origin of the bulge's structure.

That lab analysis is vital, but it's the observatory that is my temple. Time is cherished.

Clouds are despised.

Photons are coveted.

I commune with the cosmos under the dome, in a dimly lit control room surrounded by two dozen computers.

The computers stream updated information about the telescope, the detector, the observed cosmic objects, the ongoing data reductions, and the local weather.

On one such trip, a renowned colleague and friend assists me.

He is a pure theorist and has never been to a large optical telescope, meaning he doesn't know one end of a telescope from the other.

I thought it would be a good idea to bring him along, but five hours after he enters the observatory, central Chile experiences a 6.5 magnitude earthquake.

The detector's optics are shaken out of alignment and several hours of data are corrupted.

I suspect my pure-theorist friend has upset the observer gods and I consider leaving him at home next time.

CTIO sits on a seven-thousand-foot mountain, above nearly twenty-five percent of Earth's air molecules. This corresponds to a twenty-five percent drop in atmospheric pressure.

These conditions dramatically improve astronomical data, though low air pressure alone doesn't ensure the high quality data necessary to draw scientific conclusions of high confidence.

An excellent night at the telescope requires the very best viewing conditions, difficult given the rising and falling air currents of Earth's turbulent atmosphere.

When in the Andes I maintain a keen eye on the flight of Andean condors. What's good for condors is bad for astrophysicists.

If I observe a condor effortlessly ascending the mountain on a warm air current I know I will have a difficult night of observing ahead.

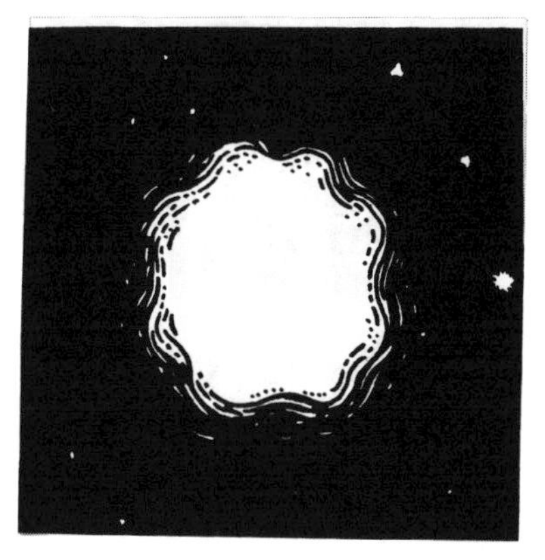

Warm air currents can turn a star's image into an undulating blob of light on the detector.

For your own safety, never tell an astrophysicist "I hope all your stars are twinkling."

The world's largest optical telescope is on Mauna Kea, in Hawaii, a mountain twice the height above sea level as Cerro Tololo.

Sitting above forty percent of Earth's atmosphere, Mauna Kea is where some of the finest ground-based observations are made. Mountains have long been considered ideal venues for cosmic inquiry.

In 1704 Sir Isaac Newton wrote about them in his treatise on optics:

"If the Theory of making Telescopes could at length be fully brought into Practice, yet there would be certain Bounds beyond which Telescopes could not perform."

"For the Air through which we look upon the Stars, is in a perpetual Tremor; as may be seen by the . . . twinkling of the fix'd Stars."

Sir Isaac continued with telescopic foresight: "The only Remedy is a most serene and quiet Air, such as may perhaps be found on the tops of the highest Mountains above the Grosser Clouds."

The thin air has its drawbacks, however.

During the long Chilean winter nights, breathing twenty-five percent less oxygen, I must maintain a level of alertness and intellectual intensity that is without comparison in everyday life.

In a normal day my mind drifts away from peak intensity during coffee breaks, lunch breaks, mail breaks, and the occasional stare out my office window.

But on the mountain I reach a self-induced state of unmatched cosmic stimulation.

I like to end the final night of my observation by listening to the finale of Beethoven's Ninth Symphony.

I soak up the twenty incessant thumps that end the fourth movement and close the observatory slit.

It makes a sound that resonates in the telescope dome with the acoustic richness of a bathroom shower.

I observe during "dark time," in which the moon is near its new phase and out of view in the night sky.

But during twilight you can see its thin crescent shape low on the horizon, framed by the layered colors of the dawn sky.

On a mountaintop, morning is a stirring panoramic sweep from the rich darkness of night to the radiant twilight on the eastern horizon.

I return home with my little piece of the universe written to a high-capacity data tape in my breast pocket.

I make two backup tapes—one secured in my checked luggage, the other left behind on the mountain.

But times have changed.

Princeton is now part of a consortium of five institutions that operate a 3.5-meter telescope at Apache Point Observatory, in New Mexico, a 9,200-foot summit near the National Solar Observatory.

The telescope is run remotely over the Internet from control rooms located at each member university.

The Princeton control room is in a specially outfitted space in the astrophysics department's basement.

In principle, the only difference between observing remotely at Apache Point and observing at Cerro Tololo is the length of the wires that connect to the back of each console.

For many observing projects, all I need do is walk for about ninety seconds from my office door to the basement observing room.

It looks, smells, and feels like a real observing room, but one cannot deny the absence of a mountain's majesty.

For better or for worse, I suppose there will come a time when I tell my grand graduate students: "Back in the old days, data didn't appear on our doorsteps."

"We traveled great distances. We ascended great mountains."

"We met the universe and its photons face-to-face."

NOTE:
An unedited version of this essay can be found in NATURAL HISTORY magazine, January 1995.

ANDREW
BIRD

The Little Yellow Post-it
by Andrew Bird

It was only my second paid gig as a professional musician.

The first was a six-week stint in the orchestra pit at an opera festival in Arkansas, for which I was paid five hundred dollars all-in.

This, however, was a good gig, playing fiddle at the Bristol Renaissance Faire in southeast Wisconsin.

I could make nearly two hundred dollars a weekend and quit my landscaping job, proving to myself and everyone else that I could make it as a professional musician.

I was to be a wandering, fiddling knave.

Not much was asked of me at first. But I did have to sign a contract that read: "I shall not misplace any phrase or expression chronologically while on premises."

This meant I couldn't tell the hurdy-gurdy player, "I dug that sweet hornpipe you just played."

And I definitely couldn't say, "Hey, play that jam again so I can rip a sweet lead over it!" (At least not within earshot of the patrons.)

The attendees ranged from families to bikers to D&D enthusiasts.

I remember one guy in a bright green felt tunic who wandered the fairgrounds with an ecstatic look on his face.

A look that seemed to say, "Yes! This is exactly how I imagined it! This is how things must've been in that vague thousand-year period between AD 800 and 1800!"

I was outfitted as a standard serf in a blousy chemise, drawstring pants, and some knock-off Vans spray-painted black. All told, it wasn't so bad, except for the floppy hat.

The hat bothered me. When I donned it I could feel my dignity get sucked under a door into a distant room.

Many of my fellow employees were shopkeepers and craftspeople who worked at Renaissance fairs year-round and lived in trailers just outside the grounds' movie set–like facade.

Others were theater majors who put on little farcical plays in their best Elizabethan accents.

I had a lot of freedom. My only directive was to wander around and play jigs and reels with various musicians who had assigned territories.

I'd jam with Evan the dulcimer player for a while, then move on to Billy the flute maker.

After that I'd sit in with Kat and Andrew, who knew all these obscure Anglo-Irish ballads.

I felt like I was my own boss, and I could even steal an afternoon nap when I was so inclined. It seemed too good to be true, so of course it was.

Someone noticed that I was enjoying my job too much and one morning I was handed a Post-it note that read:

"Privy line 2:00."

I understood right away what this economical directive meant.

I was to play jigs, reels, and French-Canadian waltzes for all the bikers and role-playing enthusiasts who'd drunk too much mead and were waiting in line for the honey bucket.

When I say "honey bucket" I mean the "drop zone" or the "Johnny on the spot." In other words, the privy.

A captive audience, yes, but preoccupied with the imperatives of their digestive tracts, not eighteenth-century Irish fiddle tunes passing for twelfth-century banquet music.

It was a particularly hot, dry, dusty day at the Bristol Renaissance Faire, and I approached my new station with a mix of dread and indignation.

I positioned myself under an oak tree about five feet from the line of impatient, unhappy, lolling patrons.

I took off one of my dusty spray-painted Vans and nudged it toward the line in optimistic hopes that someone might tip me.

No luck, so I launched into a rousing version of "Captain Rock."

There was no response, save a few glances of nonacknowledgment.

A few rolled eyes that said, "Oh, there's a fiddler."

If I had been a lawn chair I'm sure the reaction would have been exactly the same: "Oh, there's a lawn chair."

And shortly thereafter: "Oh, I shouldn't have drunk so much mead. I hope this line speeds up."

I was halfway through the "Beatrice Reel" when an excruciating jolt of pain shot through my left arm. I couldn't move my fingers.

It was like someone had injected gruel into my forearm.

I stopped playing and found a spot to lie down at the edge of the grounds. I tried to imagine a future for myself without the violin, but I couldn't. How was I going to pay my rent?

For the next five to six years I struggled with tendinitis.

And I noticed that when I was in a musical situation that had little value or the slightest whiff of futility, or, most important, when I wasn't in control, my arm stopped working.

I'm not suggesting that my tendinitis was psychosomatic. I'd played violin eight to ten hours a day for most of my life and it'd taken its toll.

But I eventually came to discover there was an upside to my ailment.

I realized I had become focused on the violin to the exclusion of much else—like poetry or Frisbee, for example.

Out of necessity I threw myself into songwriting. You don't really need to play an instrument to write a song.

And I owe it all to that little yellow Post-it note.

ARTHUR
JONES

Oakley Street
by Arthur Jones

I used to be a better person. I grew up in a Baptist family and we lived by simple rules. We didn't lie or cheat or drive over the speed limit or watch PG-13 movies.

We did unto others as we would have them do unto us. We believed as a rule that people were inherently good.

Then, in my early twenties, I met Ms. Stepowy, an old Ukrainian lady who destroyed my faith in humanity.

Ms. Stepowy came into my life during my second year living in Chicago.

My first year had been spent in an apartment that felt like a murder scene prior to cleanup. It was dark and run-down with low ceilings and floors painted bloodred.

My roommate was a depressed, recovering heroin addict who spent his days sitting on the edge of his bed, looking out the window, chain-smoking.

Adding to the unpleasantness was the location: on Western Avenue, probably the busiest, dirtiest street in the entire city.

Late one night, when I was returning home, someone whipped a beer bottle at me from a moving car.

I managed to duck, but the bottle smashed against the wall, filling the hood of my coat with broken glass.

My friend Josh was new to town, so we decided to look for a place together in Ukrainian Village.

It was a neighborhood populated by elderly Eastern Europeans that was quickly being gentrified by hipsters looking for cheap rent and authentic-seeming old-man bars.

A rental agency set us up with a big, sunny apartment on the first floor of a house on a quiet, tree-lined street. The building was owned by Ms. Stepowy.

Ms. Stepowy was a heavyset woman in her late seventies with knee-length gray hair that she kept tucked under a head scarf. Her face was speckled with moles and warts.

She always wore a heavy coat over several layers of clothing, even on hot summer days, making her look (and smell) like an anthropomorphic pile of sweat-soaked laundry.

She lived directly above us, which was a little worrisome, but the rental agency swore she wasn't going to give us a hard time.

This proved to be untrue almost immediately. A few days after moving in I got a phone call from someone at the agency.

"Ms. Stepowy wants to evict you. You've violated your lease agreement." "What do you mean?" I asked.

"The lease clearly states no dogs or cats." I was dumbfounded. Josh and I had no pets. I called Ms. Stepowy to figure out what was going on.

"You have dog!" she exclaimed. I remember thinking that her impenetrable accent made her sound like a decrepit version of Natasha from the *Rocky and Bullwinkle* cartoons.

Next I expected her to accuse us of harboring moose and squirrel. "You very bad boy. I hear dog in apartment."

"That's impossible," I replied. "We don't have a dog." "You no tell truth."

Early that evening I let Ms. Stepowy waddle into the apartment to look for dogs. She found nothing.

"I sorry," she said. "I make mistake. No dog." "Why did you think we had one?" I asked.

"Long time ago, dog lived here and made mess," she said, pointing to a discolored spot on the living room floor. "Bad dog."

"But you said you heard a dog?"

Ms. Stepowy quickly corrected me. "I no hear dog, I have dog feeling. You understand what it's like to have dog feeling?"

I shook my head. I didn't understand what it was like to have "dog feeling."

But I imagined it to be a superpower, similar to Spider-Man's spidey sense, that tingled whenever a dog was about to piss on a hardwood floor.

On her way out, Ms. Stepowy squeezed my forearm. "You good boy," she whispered, giving me a wink.

Things only got weirder from there. Ms. Stepowy frequently claimed that we boiled rotting meat late at night, the smell of which made her vomit in bed.

She accused us of using a mysterious "exercise machine" that shook the house so violently it, again, made her vomit.

She always was vomiting and it always was our fault.

Once, believing wild animals were loose in her bedroom, she left a message on our answering machine, shrieking, "It eat me! It eat me!" over and over.

She paused periodically to see if Josh or I would pick up. When we didn't, she said, "Maybe I go die now," in a small, pitiful voice, and hung up.

It was the most bewildering and hilarious thing we'd ever heard, and we spent weeks playing it for anyone who'd listen.

But as ridiculous as the message was, I still checked on Ms. Stepowy the next day. I couldn't help it—she was old and alone, and I felt for her.

Josh couldn't understand this. He thought Ms. Stepowy was malicious and insane, so he shut the door in her face and hung up whenever she called.

There was part of me that wanted to do the same, but I'd been conditioned to respect my elders, and it was a hard habit to break. So I was patient to a fault and even ran errands for her.

Eventually I grew so concerned about Ms. Stepowy that I asked the rental agency to put me in touch with her next of kin. They gave me a number for her daughter, Nadia.

The day I called, Bill, Nadia's husband, picked up. He told me he and Nadia were concerned, but they were living in rural Alaska with their ten kids and weren't really in a position to help.

As if that weren't enough of a hindrance, they were also legally blind.

At a certain point during the conversation, Bill asked me what I did for a living. I told him I was working as a Web designer. "Me too!" he exclaimed.

I almost dropped the phone. I knew Beethoven was deaf when he wrote his Ninth Symphony.

And the drummer in Def Leppard was missing an arm, but I couldn't begin to imagine a blind man designing a Web site.

"It's easy!" he said. "I just taught myself HTML."

The first thing I did after I got off the phone was sprint to my computer to look at Bill's site. It mostly consisted of links to Alaskan wildlife Web sites and photos of his family.

The text was a dozen different colors and sizes and many of the images were set at the wrong width, making them look like reflections in a funhouse mirror.

A few days later I told Ms. Stepowy I had contacted her family. "They don't care," she scoffed. "They bad people."

It occurred to me that Nadia and Bill might have moved to Alaska to get as far away from Ms. Stepowy as possible. Maybe she wasn't senile. Maybe she'd always been nuts.

One night in July the phone rang. "Help!" Ms. Stepowy croaked. "I have heart attack! I maybe die!"

I ran upstairs to find Ms. Stepowy reclining in an easy chair with a washcloth on her forehead. She looked fine but claimed she was having chest pains.

She said she was out of her medicine and insisted I call her doctor to ask for more pills. She claimed that if she didn't get her pills she might die.

"She's been bugging me all day," the doctor huffed angrily. "I'm not giving her a refill." *Click.*

I examined the half-dozen empty pill bottles on the table next to Ms. Stepowy—all from different pharmacies, all prescribed by different doctors, all for the same drug: Xanax.

In high school I'd worked at a pharmacy and learned how addicts "double dipped," getting different doctors to prescribe the same medication.

Xanax is a highly addictive, antianxiety drug that causes all sorts of problems when overused, including disorientation and nausea.

Josh and I hadn't been jiggling the vomit out of her with our imaginary, earthquake-inducing exercise machine. She'd been doing it to herself by binging on pills.

Ms. Stepowy's doctor had figured out her scheme and cut her off. She wasn't a helpless old lady at all—she was a junkie, who was trying to play me by faking a heart attack.

"I can't help you," I told her, heading for the door. "If you go, I die," she said, clutching her chest dramatically.

"If you are really having a heart attack, then I'm calling 911," I said. "The paramedics can help you."

"No," Ms. Stepowy pleaded. "I don't want them in my house."

"Why not?" "What if they black?" she replied, her voice filled with terror.

I'd often heard Ms. Stepowy mutter about the black and Puerto Rican teenagers who hung out on our corner. Now she was terrified by the possibility of having a black guy in her house.

Worse, she assumed as a white guy I would understand this, not call 911, and then help her beg for more Xanax.

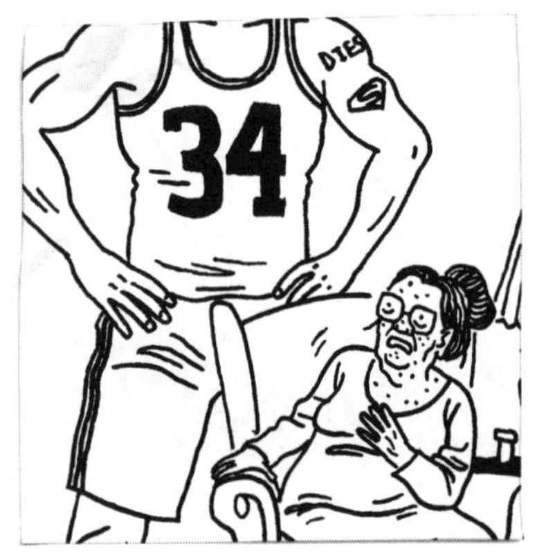

I called 911 hoping Shaquille O'Neal would show up and give her a real heart attack.

"You very bad boy," Ms. Stepowy told me. We scowled at each other in silence until the ambulance arrived.

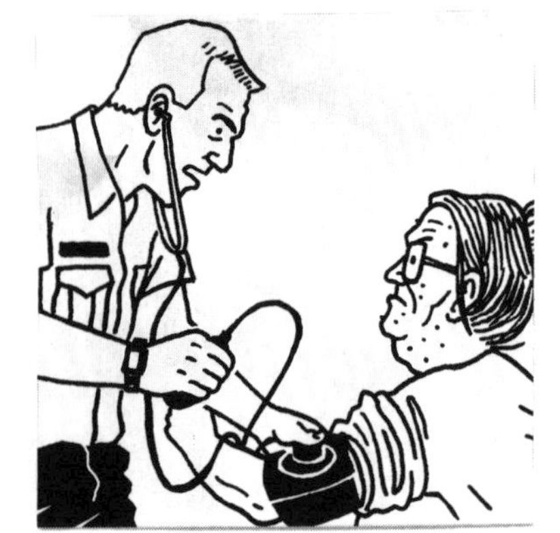

None of the paramedics were black and of course they found nothing wrong with Ms. Stepowy.

Our final months in the apartment were bananas. Ms. Stepowy accused us of doing drugs, not paying rent, flooding the basement using a hose from our sink, and constantly making her vomit.

She called the police so often it became a joke between us and the cops. When we moved out at the end of our lease, she kept our security deposit for no reason.

Losing the money was reason enough to feel cheated, but for me, it felt far worse having taken pity on an old woman who in turn only took advantage of me.

It made me want something I'd never really wanted before: revenge.

Josh and I became obsessed with suing Ms. Stepowy. We filed the necessary paperwork and on the day of our hearing acted like we were appearing before the Supreme Court.

We put on our best thrift store suits and brought photos of our clean apartment to submit as evidence.

Not that any of it was necessary: Ms. Stepowy didn't even bother to show up; we won automatically. It took a long to time to collect our money, but eventually we did.

A year or so later, while biking past the old apartment, I saw a family walking hand in hand in a single-file line, like a chain of circus elephants.

At the front was the father, wearing sunglasses and tapping the sidewalk with a white cane. It was Bill, Ms. Stepowy's son-in-law—I recognized him from the photos on the Web site.

As I watched him and his family pass, I wondered how Ms. Stepowy was doing. For a split second I even considered stopping him to see if she was OK. Then I changed my mind.

"She can go fuck herself," I said to myself as I biked away.

JONATHAN
GOLDSTEIN

All Happy Families
by Jonathan Goldstein

My sister was pushing forty when she announced her pregnancy.

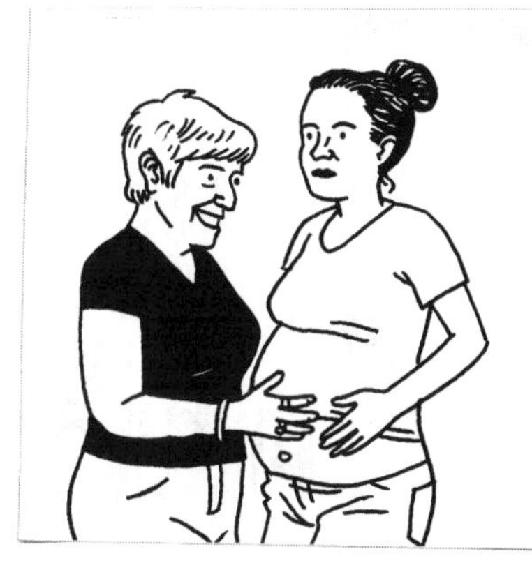

"It's a miracle," my mother said. Dina Goldstein had had me in her teens; she believed in early starts.

Rising at 5:00 a.m. to dust ceiling fans and fireplace logs, she was sprung from the mold of shtetl women past who cleaned, loved, and worried with great ferocity.

Which is to say, she'd been waiting to be a grandmother since her twenties.

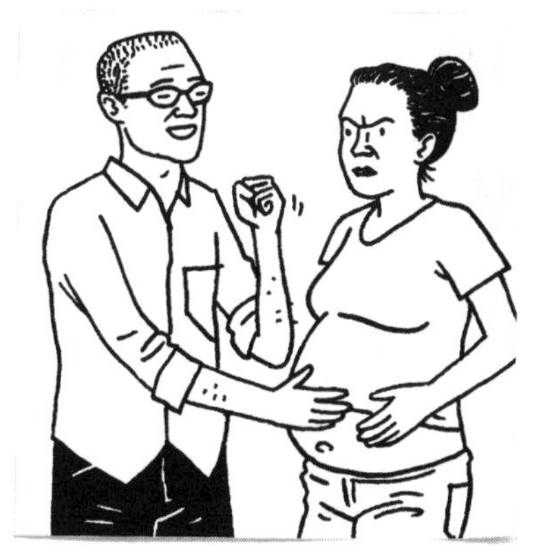

And which is also to say, with my sister's good news, the pressure was off me.

We're not the closest family in the world—get-togethers are usually reserved for funerals and the Jewish high holidays, both equally mirthless affairs.

On the blessed day of the baby's arrival, we all meet up at my sister's hospital room.

But just now, I've never been in a room where so many members of my family are this happy all at once.

Usually, maybe one or two are happy at any given time, while the rest hold down the fort.

Remaining dyspeptic and dysphoric, or boldly struggling to maintain a nice, even level of dispiritedness.

Tolstoy once wrote that every unhappy family is unhappy in its own way, and happy families are all alike.

This is not so, as is evidenced by my father, who is smilingly biting into a home-brought chicken sandwich while seated atop an upturned wastepaper basket.

And my mother, who is rubbing disinfectant soap onto her lips in preparation to kiss the newborn.

We all stand around for hours, happily staring at the baby and clutching our chests.

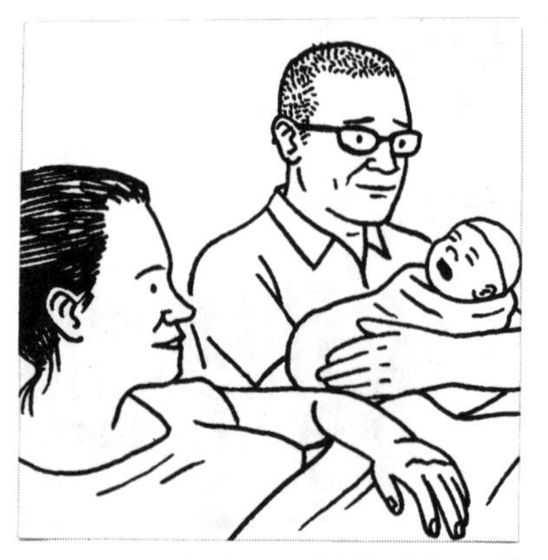

How strange to feel yourself falling in love with someone you've only just met.

And how endlessly fascinating it is to watch someone getting used to being alive.

Though perhaps even more fascinating is watching someone getting used to being a part of our family.

The male pattern baldness that starts at twelve.

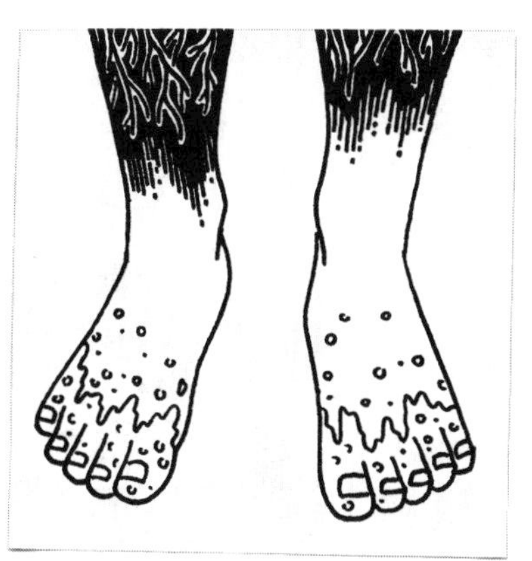

The foot fungus that rises up to the thighs and the hemorrhoids that descend to the ankles.

Not to mention the messy eating.

Legend has it that one time my father kept an egg noodle hanging from his lower lip for the duration of the July Fourth weekend.

If he could have only lasted a few days longer he might have ended up on the Johnny Carson show, seated on the couch alongside the guy who had hiccupped for forty years.

But to look at him—Justin Mitchell, so little and brand-new—and to even think these things feels wrong somehow. I shoo away these thoughts, and try to think only positively.

"May he enjoy nothing but happiness," I intone. Not wanting to draw attention, I intone to myself. "Days without embarrassment. Days without pain."

Or at least seven days without pain, at which point he will have the flesh at the end of his penis shorn off.

After which Dixie cups of schnapps and honey cake will be served.

The night before Justin's bris, I can't sleep.

After the last bris I attended, it was days before I could pry my hands out of my pockets.

At 6:00 a.m., I decide to just get out of bed and make my way over to the synagogue.

I'm the first guest to arrive, so I hang out with the mohel. As he prepares his tools, we make small talk, and at a certain point, he tells me why he got into "moheling."

But before he can get very far, and with my heart racing because I know it might be the only time I'll ever get the chance to use this line on an actual mohel, I blurt out, "For the tips?"

The mohel doesn't laugh, which doesn't make sense to me. The context is perfect, and my timing, impeccable.

I conclude that to be a good mohel, you must always be on guard against the peril of shaking with laughter.

In other cultures such sure-handed individuals might become jewel thieves.

With their steady hands they could become expert bomb deactivators.

Or even one of those guys who teaches you how to paint landscapes on TV.

But not the Jews. If you've a son impervious to backfiring cars and air horns, it's off to moheling college. Or, if you're a little "off"—medical school.

The family shows up and things begin. I have been honored with the task of holding the baby during the procedure.

I am later shown a photo of me, Justin in my arms, looking off to the side as though turning away from a horror film. Which, in fact, I am.

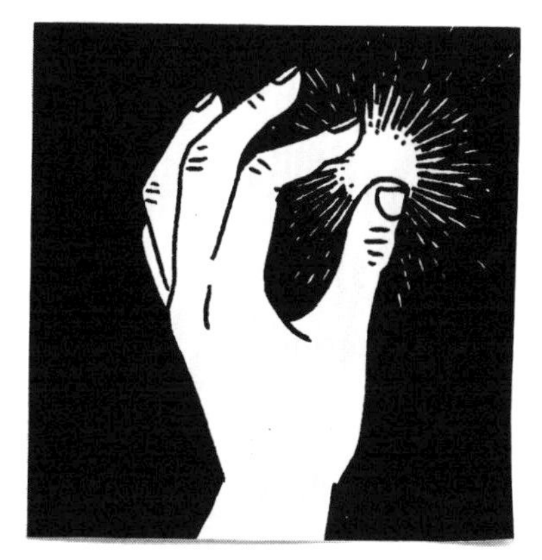

To keep steady, I imagine I am holding the future itself. Which, in fact, I am.

And so the future begins: Mother's Day—Justin's first—and when I show up to the Greek restaurant, my family is already at the table.

We focus all of our attention on Justin.

We constantly worry for his comfort and safety, and so every time he shifts in his baby seat, we clutch our hearts and mop the sweat from our brows with fistfuls of napkin.

"I love him so much it hurts," my sister says, her hand on her mouth.

"Me, too," my father says. "It physically hurts."

"It's like someone is beating me with sandbags," my mother says.

"With me it's more of a stabbing," my father counters.

"I love him so much," my aunt says, "it's like having a serrated blade corkscrewed into my side."

Not one to be outdone, my sister weighs in: "I love him so much I feel like I'm drowning in love and can't breathe."

She demonstrates the sensation by making gagging and gasping noises while scratching at the air.

As we eat, my father accidentally tips a plate of olive oil into his lap.

Pretty soon afterward, my aunt somehow manages to drip the wax from the candelabra onto her pants.

When I look over at my mother, she is wearing a bib of smeared tzatziki sauce across the chest of her black turtleneck.

Ironically, the baby proves to be the neatest eater of us all. Truly, it feels like he is the best of us all.

I look over at him and he smiles a little smile at me that fills my heart with so much love.

It's as though I have had my eyes sprayed with acid.

And my heart stabbed with a salad fork.

Wincing, I reach across the table for another soothing spoonful of *taramosalata*, and as I do, I drag my jacket sleeve through a puddle of spilled gravy.

It feels like the final touch-up to a happy family portrait.

BETH
LISICK

Lurch of a Lifetime
by Beth Lisick

I had to get out of San Jose. It was embarrassing to stay in the city where I grew up when San Francisco was only forty-five minutes away.

At the time, I was a baker at a Sicilian place run by a former bank robber.

And it was getting hard for me to drink four beers, smoke half a pack of cigarettes, go to bed at midnight, and wake up at 3:00 a.m. to work every day.

So I hatched a plan to get a regular office job in San Francisco and get on with my life. I mean, I was almost twenty-four.

When I first moved to the city, I lived in a tiny room underneath the staircase in my brother's apartment.

I also slept over a lot at my boyfriend Morgan's studio apartment, where most of my stuff was stored.

That's were I was the night before my first job interview, at a temp agency in San Francisco.

I probably should have stayed at my brother's, but Morgan and I were breaking up and therefore inseparable.

About 2:00 a.m., we were awakened by the sound of the building's fire alarm, followed immediately by screaming sirens.

We hopped down from the sleeping loft, threw on some clothes, and fled into the street.

It was a scene out there. The bars were just closing down and the streets were packed with people watching the flames on our roof.

There was a tap on my shoulder. It was one of the bartenders from the Ajax, the bar across the street. He asked us if we wanted to go inside and watch the action from the bar.

We drank tequila after tequila and waited to see if our stuff would be spared.

This was the first time I ever drank myself through a life semi-drama and it felt great. Like I was doing important work.

Around 5:00 a.m., we were allowed back into the apartment, very drunk. The whole place smelled like smoke but at least our stuff was OK.

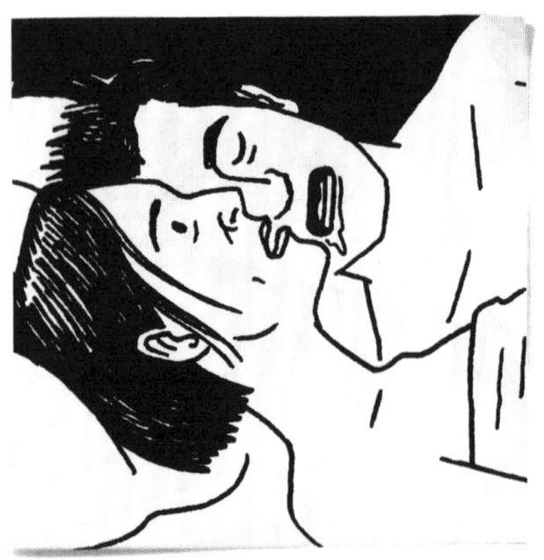

It wasn't until we crawled back up to the mattress that I remembered. My interview!

I jumped down and set the tiny travel alarm clock for seven and kept it downstairs so I would have to get up to turn it off.

All those years of teenage sports training and professional baking really paid off. After two hours of sleep, it was a snap for me to go on autopilot first thing in the morning.

I discovered I was even able to dress myself in a way that was not natural to me, digging into a box and pulling out an outfit that my mom had gotten me for Christmas.

To call it a jumpsuit doesn't seem quite accurate.

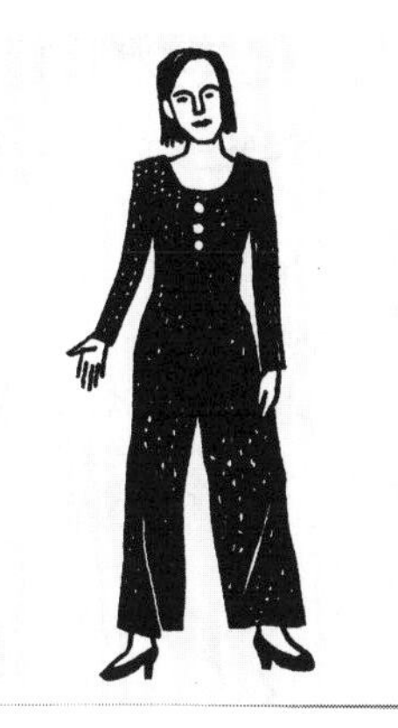

It was a one-piece polyblend outfit in navy blue with small white flowers. It zipped up the back and had long, tapering sleeves and wide, floppy legs.

I thought of it as a "nice outfit" that would make me look employable.

I jammed my pickup truck through rush hour traffic with little time to spare, but was way too cheap to pay for the parking garage next to the place I was going.

My friend's brother always said only tourists paid for parking in the city, and I would not be a tourist. I was going to live in this city and have a real job.

I found a meter about six blocks away, emptied whatever change I had in my ashtray into it, and sprinted down the street.

During this sprint, it became clear that I was hungover in a way that was new to me.

My head was pounding, my muscles were rubbery, my mouth was dry and cracked.

I felt like I was going to have a seizure up until the very moment I entered the building, when I had another new experience. Something called "flop sweat."

However, I was quite impressed by my own résumé and was sure they would be too.

Did I temp at my friend's stepdad's orthodontist office during winter break of 1985?

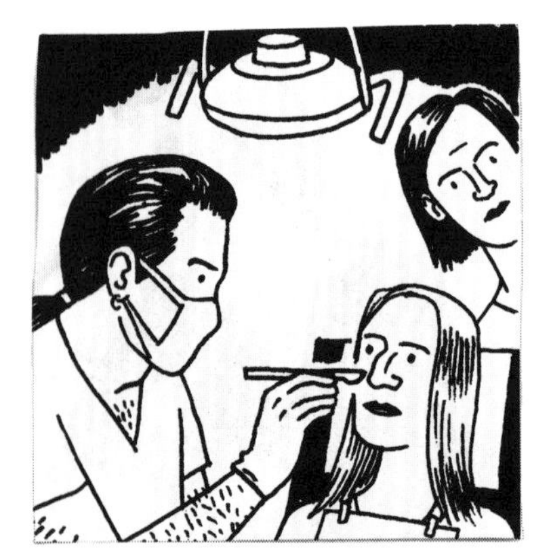

Did I later move to a job as file manager at the plastic surgeon's office down the street on a part-time basis after school in the spring of '86 at the rate of five dollars an hour?

Had I been responsible for every single hamburger bun and piece of apple pie at a very well-known and semi-historic diner? I had. Thank you for asking.

My résumé made it seem like I could have been a divorcée in my midforties.

The office lady seemed nice and for a moment I thought I would tell her about the fire. Get some sympathy points.

Nah, I decided. Not my style. Apparently my style was to show up smelling like booze in a Laura Ashley onesie.

First up was the typing test, in which I was panicked to discover I would be judged on speed and accuracy.

I pressed the space bar to begin, but my hands were trembling terribly. I could barely hit the keys.

As the time ticked down, the number on the "words per minute" display went into complete free fall, from 38 words per minute to 37, 36, 35, 34.

With each second I didn't type, an electronic blip, like the one in Atari Pong, came out of the computer.

Soon I was down to twelve words per minute. *Pong, pong, pong, pong.*

Clearly, the best way to resolve this was to get up and leave the building. Without telling anyone.

I stood up, pointed my index finger toward the elevator button, and shuffled toward it.

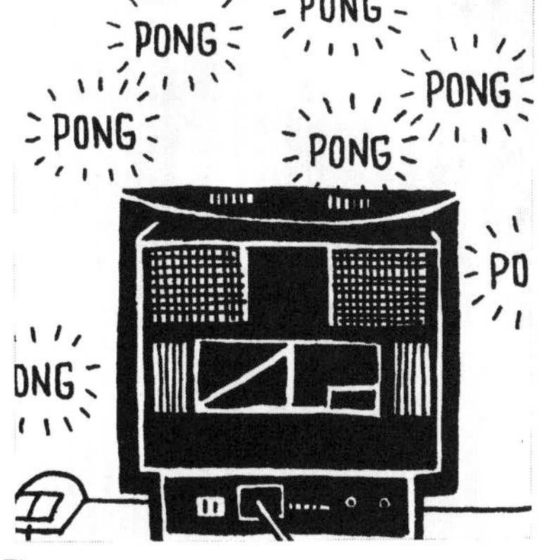

The computer ponged away, tattling on me.

So focused was I on the elevator doors that I startled easily when the nice lady came up and touched the small of my back.

Was everything OK? Was I done with my test already?

Instead of telling her about the fire now, which would seem like a lie or else why wouldn't I have mentioned it earlier, my mouth replied with something a little less true.

"I think I am having an allergic reaction to my medication."

I was on no medication and therefore not quite prepared for the question that came next. "What kind of medication?"

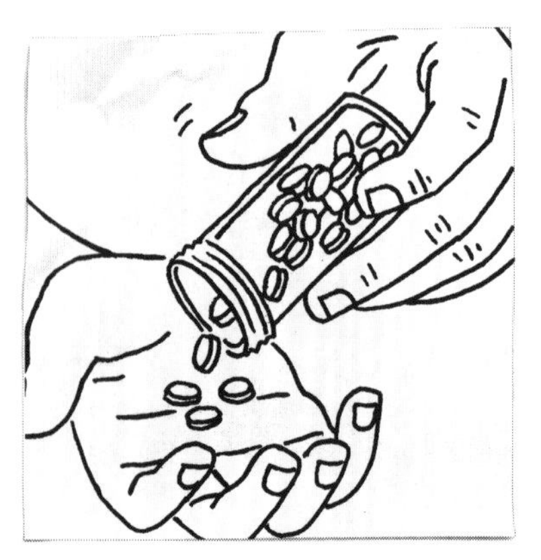

At the time, my boyfriend's mother was having a thyroid issue. Why not me too?

"Thyroid."

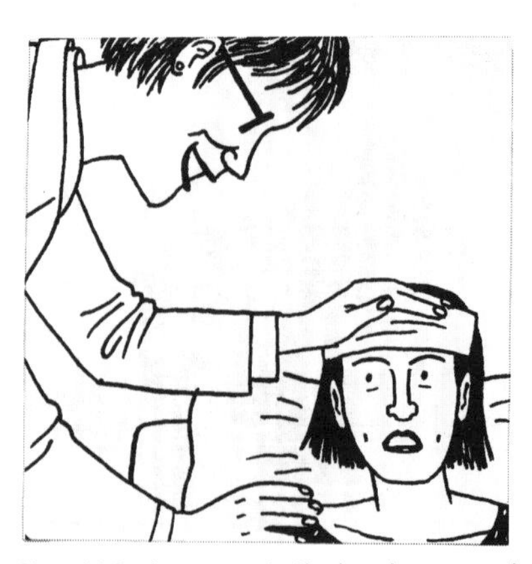

She whisked me away to the break room and told me to lie down, putting a cool washcloth on my head.

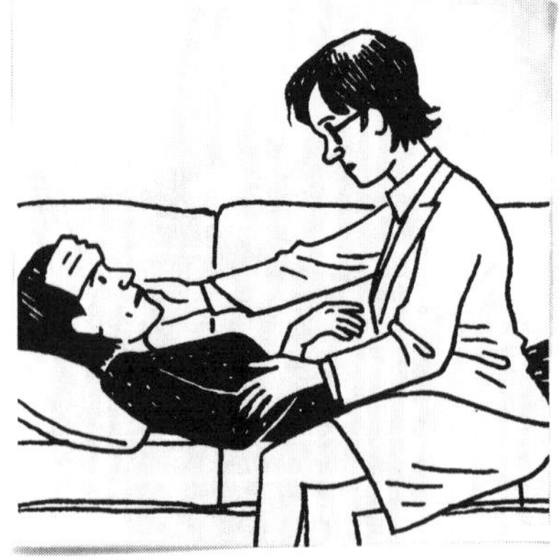

"You look clammy."

"I feel clammy."

She turned off the lights and I heard whispering outside the door.

When the voices went away, I got up and headed to the elevator.

Busted again.

"You should really stay here and rest. Marcy's on her way from upstairs. Her sister is on thyroid meds too."

I was looking at my feet. "I just want to go. My brother works down the street. He's coming to get me."

Part of that was true. He did work down the street, but in this age before cell phones, I don't know how they thought I had gotten hold of him to come pick me up so quickly.

I shuffled into the elevator and then back to my truck, on which there was a parking ticket. I was suddenly overcome by the powerful urge to take a shit.

I just didn't have it in me to stop at a local business and deal with talking to someone, pretending to purchase something, or getting a special key.

I drove across town to my brother's apartment, nearly hallucinating from this disturbing glandular funk of dehydration, humiliation, and gastric distress.

After fumbling with his keys at the front gate for what must have been a solid minute, it became clear I needed another plan.

The closest place was a church. Not just a church, but a Spanish mission. I remember my parents telling me that the doors to Catholic churches were always unlocked.

But when I found the door locked, it occurred to me that maybe they were being metaphorical in hopes I would return to going to mass at some point.

I turned to the curb. A tour bus was idling out front and the passengers had just begun disembarking.

Quickly, I slipped into line and filed into the dark basilica with them, breaking away from the pack when I was safe inside.

The back-zippered outfit was nearly impossible to undo.

But after some struggle it eventually dropped to the floor.

I plopped onto the toilet and let loose, feeling like myself for the first time that day.

The End

ACKNOWLEDGMENTS

I'd like to thank Jason Bitner for counseling me throughout this project, from assisting me with the book proposal to helping scan hundreds of drawings, I owe you many a Maker's on the rocks; Starlee Kine, my favorite writer, for collaborating with me on the Post-it Note Reading Series and being such a generous advocate and loyal friend over the years; David Wilcox, my favorite Texan, for the late-night chats and editorial wisdom; Cyrus Highsmith, my favorite typographer, for letting me use his font, Benton Sans, and counseling me on the book's design; K. J. Martinet for all her valuable production assistance; Karl Ackermann for his enthusiasm on and off the court and for making me buy that crappy microwave; my family: John, Karen, and Miriam; Jud Laghi, my agent, for all the elbow grease; my patient and insightful editors Becky Cole and Anna Sternoff at Penguin; Joshua Gleason for letting me draw his face; Simen Johan for being a great studio mate; and all the authors who so generously gave their abundant talents to this project.

Finally and most of all, I'd like to acknowledge Agnes Bolt, for being so lovely, feisty, and supportive. Like the thump of a dachshund's tail my heart beats for you.

ABOUT THE CONTRIBUTORS

Since age four, Chicago-based songwriter/performer **Andrew Bird** has been playing music ranging from classical to early country blues. He has spent the past thirteen years writing pop music infused with unconventional violin, glockenspiel, guitar, and his trademark whistling. He's released eleven albums, most recently the widely lauded *Noble Beast* (2009), and is currently recording his next album due out in the spring of 2012.

Arthur Bradford's first book, *Dogwalker*, was published by Knopf in 2001. He is the creator and director of the documentary news series *How's Your News?*, which has been broadcast on HBO and MTV. His first children's book, *Walrus and Slugs Together,* is due out from McSweeney's in the spring of 2011.

Neil deGrasse Tyson has written nine books including *New York Times* bestseller *Death by Black Hole and Other Cosmic Quandaries* and *The Pluto Files: The Rise and Fall of America's Favorite Planet*. He hosts the PBS program *NOVA scienceNOW* and was voted "Sexiest Astrophysicist Alive" by *People* magazine in 2000. Tyson is the first occupant of the Frederick P. Rose Directorship of the Hayden Planetarium and lives with his wife and two children in New York City.

Daniel Engber is a senior editor at *Slate*. His scientific method for distracting free-throw shooters in the NBA was featured in the *New York Times Magazine*'s "Year in Ideas" issue for 2005, and his Web site, Crying While Eating, was featured on *The Tonight Show*. His work has been anthologized in the Best of Technology Writing series, and made him a finalist for a James Beard Foundation Award in 2010 and the winner of a Sex-Positive Journalism Award in 2008.

Jonathan Goldstein is the host and producer of CBC Radio's *WireTap*, and the author, most recently, of *Ladies and Gentlemen, the Bible!*

John Hodgman is a writer, humorist, and former minor television celebrity. He is the author of *The Areas of My Expertise* and *More Information Than You Require* and hosts the podcast Judge John Hodgman. To keep an update of his activities visit www.areasofmyexpertise.com.

Arthur Jones is an animator, graphic designer, illustrator, and writer who was born in Texas, raised in Missouri, and currently lives in Brooklyn, New York. You can see more of his work at www.byarthurjones.com.

Starlee Kine, cocreator of the Post-it Note Reading series from which this book originated, is a frequent contributor to public radio's *This American Life*. Her writing has appeared in numerous publications including the *New York Times Magazine* and *Wired*. She is currently working on her first book, entitled *It IS Your Fault* for Riverhead Books.

Chuck Klosterman has published four nonfiction books, an anthology of his journalism, and the novel *Downtown Owl*. He has written for *GQ*, *Esquire*, *SPIN*, the *New York Times Magazine*, *Washington Post*, *ESPN*, *The Believer*, *The Guardian*, the *Akron Beacon Journal*, and the *Forum of Fargo-Moorhead*. His second novel, *The Visible Man*, will be released in the fall of 2011.

Laura Krafft is an artist/writer/performer from Evanston, Illinois, whose primary media are television and embroidery.

Beth Lisick is the author of four books, including the *New York Times* bestseller *Everybody Into the Pool*. She cofounded the Porchlight Storytelling Series in San Francisco and occasionally appears on stages and screens.

Marie Lorenz is an artist living in Brooklyn. She currently teaches printmaking at the Yale University School of Art. She has exhibited nationally and internationally, including solo projects at Artpace in San Antonio, Texas; Ikon Gallery in Birmingham, England; Locust Projects in Miami, Florida; and the Jack Hanley Gallery in New York. In an ongoing artwork entitled *The Tide and Current Taxi*, she ferries people around New York City in her handmade boat.

David Rakoff is the author of several books, the most recent being *Half Empty*. A regular contributor to public radio's *This American Life*, he has written for the *New York Times*, *GQ*, *Salon*, *Wired*, the *Wall Street Journal*, and *Outside*, among numerous other publications.

David Rees is an artisanal pencil sharpener. From 2001 to 2008, he wrote *Get Your War On*.

Mary Roach is the author of *Stiff*, *Bonk*, and, most recently, *Packing for Mars*. She currently has no pets.

Kristen Schaal is a comedian, writer, and actor. Some highlights: *The Daily Show* with Jon Stewart, *Flight of the Conchords*, *Toy Story 3*, and her own Comedy Central Presents special. She is coauthor of *The Sexy Book of Sexy Sex* with Rich Blomquist.

Jeff Simmermon is a writer and storyteller who has contributed to *This American Life* and regularly appears onstage at the Moth and other storytelling shows around New York. He thinks he may have been contacted by an extraterrestrial intelligence a few times in his early twenties and quietly panics that God is disappointed in him when he hasn't created enough art. Jeff also runs a blog packed full of stories, art, and other weirdness at www.andiamnotlying.com.

Andrew Solomon is a lecturer in psychiatry at Weill Cornell Medical College, where the *ndeup* is often invoked but seldom prescribed. His most recent book, *The Noonday Demon: An Atlas of Depression*—which propelled him quite unexpectedly into close encounters with the Senegalese spirit world—won the National Book Award and was a finalist for the Pulitzer Prize. His next book, to be published in 2012, is *Far from the Tree: A Lineage of Love*. He lives in London and New York with his husband and son.

Hannah Tinti is the author of *Animal Crackers*, and cofounder and editor in chief of *One Story* magazine. Her bestselling novel, *The Good Thief*, is a *New York Times* Notable Book of the Year, winner of the John Sargent Sr. First Novel Prize, and a recipient of the American Library Association's Alex Award. Recently she joined the cast of NPR's *Selected Shorts*.

David Wilcox is a writer whose work has appeared on public radio's *This American Life* and in the pages of the *Chicago Reader*. He currently lives in Los Angeles, but you can find him online at www.thisisdavidwilcox.com.